A Priceless Treasure

Sister Teresa McDonald

Pioneer Sister of St Joseph

1838 – 1876

Marie Crowley

ATF Theology
Adelaide
2016

This book is dedicated

to the memory

of

Sister Teresa McDonald

Acknowledgements

This book is largely the result of the desire of many Sisters of St Joseph to know more about Sister Teresa McDonald, the founding Provincial of the Sisters of St Joseph in the diocese of Bathurst. Thank you to all the Sisters for their interest, encouragement and support during the researching and writing of her story.

My special thanks go to all those who assisted me in particular ways: Mrs Jennie Sach (great grandniece of Sister Teresa), Stefania Di Maria (Archivist, Archdiocese of Perth), Roslyn Kennedy (Archivist, Sisters of St Joseph North Sydney), Sister Ann Leesue (Archivist, Sisters of St Joseph, Adelaide), Sister Patricia Thompson (Archives, Sisters of St Joseph North Sydney), Sister Philomena Kalmund (Researcher), Sister Mary Murphy (Manager, St Joseph's Heritage and Conference Centre, Perthville), Mrs Kath Behrendt, Mrs Robyn Finau and Mrs Sandy Leaitua (technical assistance).

My particular acknowledgement and sincere thanks go to the following Sisters of St Joseph: Marie White, Margaret McKenna, Margaret Tomlinson and Marie Foale for their careful reading, comments, suggestions and encouragement.

I am sincerely grateful to Sister Monica Cavanagh, Congregational Leader of the Sisters of St Joseph of the Sacred Heart, who commissioned the project.

My hope is that this work will bring to life Sister Teresa McDonald—a pioneer Sister of St Joseph, a faithful and courageous woman who richly deserves those words spoken about her by Mary MacKillop—'a priceless treasure.'

Foreword

It is appropriate that this book, *A Priceless Treasure: Sister Teresa McDonald Pioneering Sister of St Joseph 1838–1876* is being launched in this Sesquicentenary year of the Sisters of St Joseph. Teresa knew both Father Julian Tenison Woods and Mary MacKillop. She imbibed their vision and dream for living the Gospel and in turn passed this same spirit on to those with whom she lived and ministered.

This book tells her story, a remarkable pioneering Sister of St Joseph. Just the eighth woman to join the newly forming Institute, she emerges within this story as a 'priceless treasure'. Her life as a Sister of St Joseph spanned just eight years yet in the telling of her life Marie Crowley enables the reader to meet a woman of gentle strength known for her compassion and kindness, her steadfastness and loyalty, her discretion and prudence. She holds a special place in the early Josephite story as the first Provincial in South Australia, as the one who knelt beside Mary MacKillop at the moment of her excommunication and the one who led the first community of the Sisters of St Joseph to Perthville, the first Josephite foundation in New South Wales. Today she lays at rest in the scenic Josephite cemetery at Perthville as a unifying symbol of an expanding Josephite story.

Doctor Marie Crowley brings to this account of Teresa's life both her skill and scholarship as author and historian. She has the wonderful gift of engaging you immediately in the story. To find Bishop Matthew Quinn kneeling and sobbing at Teresa's death bed, immediately makes you want to know more. Who is this woman who brought forth this response at the time of her death? It is a story which touches deeply one's emotions as you encounter Teresa the woman struggling with ill health, bearing both the delight and burden of leadership, reaching out with 'gentleness and kindliness of manner' to the Sisters and to the people among whom she lived. One experiences both the inner and outer realities of her journey as she travels through rough passages and calm waters always attentive to the ever watchful loving presence of God.

I trust that each one who reads Teresa's story will be inspired by her wisdom, her beautiful respectful manner and her capacity to remain faithful through the many varying experiences that life presented. May her life speak to you the reader and give you the courage to believe in your own capacity to speak your truth as she did and to know that you too are a 'priceless treasure'.

Sister Monica Cavanagh
Congregational Leader
Sisters of St Joseph of the Sacred Heart

Table of Contents

Abbreviations

Unless otherwise noted, archival material cited in the text is from the collection held by the Sisters of St Joseph in the archives at St Joseph's Convent, North Sydney, and /or St Joseph's Heritage and Conference Centre, Perthville.

ASSJA   Archives of the Sisters of St Joseph, Adelaide.
DBA   Diocese of Bathurst Archives

1

The Vale

The bishop knelt by her bedside, head bowed, rosary beads in hand. His gentle words of consolation and hope mingled with the official prayers for the dying that filled the room. Though her life had been draining away for months, he had clung to the hope that she would recover. Not now. Her shallow, irregular breathing could not last. He took up the prayers for the dying giving them out strongly as he blessed the dying woman with holy water. Suddenly, he was overcome and still kneeling, broke into deep sobs. It was some time before Bishop Matthew Quinn finally stood and left the room.[1]

And the next day the telegraph wire took the message: 'Sister Provincial died half past ten o'clock yesterday evening.'[2]

Her friends in far off Brisbane mourned her passing: 'Our God I am sure has a beautiful place for her. She was such a darling creature. She was too kind . . . she was so gentle.'[3] '. . . our dear loved Sister was so good. Ah, if you were to know her as long as I did and know her goodness.'[4] And in St Ignatius Church, Adelaide, a requiem Mass

---

1. This account of Bishop Quinn at the bedside of the dying Sister Teresa McDonald is taken from a letter written by Sister Joseph Dwyer to Sister Calasanctius Howley, 21.1.1876. Although Sister Joseph was not present at Teresa's death, the Sisters who were in the room at that time would have given her an accurate account of the Provincial's death. Some details of the account are confirmed in the eulogy given by Father McAuliffe at Teresa's funeral.
2. Telegram from Sister Mary Hyacinth, St Joseph's Convent The Vale, dispatched from Bathurst Station to Sister Calasanctius, St Joseph's Convent Adelaide received at Norwood Station, 14 January 1876.
3. Sister Agnes Smith to Mother Mary MacKillop, 16.1.1876.
4. Sister Josephine McMullen to MacKillop, January, 1876.

was celebrated and the Office of the Dead chanted by 'the Bishop, the Archdeacon, and several other priests' for 'poor, dear Sister Teresa.'[5]

The death of the Provincial of the Sisters of St Joseph, Sister Teresa McDonald, at The Vale on 13 January 1876 at the age of thirty-seven was a tragic happening.[6] But it was more than that. It was a tragedy intensified by the circumstances of the previous months and by the events of the first days of 1876. Teresa died in the midst of upheaval and uncertainty among her Sisters resulting from the desire of the bishop of Bathurst, Matthew Quinn, to take over the governance of the Institute and his subsequent directions in that regard. Nothing could have required her presence and leadership more clearly and urgently. Yet the Provincial was dead.

The happenings in the small village of The Vale, near Bathurst in New South Wales on that fateful day in January 1876 have their genesis in far off Scotland and stretch to three Australian colonies. Their more immediate beginnings took place at The Vale on 16 July 1872. That was the day Teresa and her three companions, Sisters Hyacinth Quinlan, Joseph Dwyer and a young lay woman Ada Braham, had finally settled into the sacristy of the little church at The Vale. It was to be their convent and the first foundation of the newly founded Australian religious order, the Sisters of St Joseph of the Sacred Heart, in New South Wales. They were there at the request of the bishop of Bathurst, Matthew Quinn, who had invited the Sisters to establish a system of Catholic education in the diocese.

But three and a half years later, when that small group had grown to some thirty-six Sisters, confusion and doubt weighted heavily upon each woman.

When the Sisters of St Joseph were founded by Father Julian Tenison Woods and Mother Mary MacKillop in South Australia in 1866, Father Woods wrote the Rule for the new group of aspiring religious. Both founders understood that the intention of that Rule was that the Institute be governed by a Sister Guardian-General. However, there was some ambiguity in the wording of the Rule. This, together with a number of other reasons, resulted in the bishop in whose diocese the Sisters worked believing that he was the properly

---

5. Howley to MacKillop, 12.1.1876. There is an error in the date on this letter.
6. Due to further research Sister Teresa's surname is given here as McDonald rather than MacDonald. The date of her birth has been confirmed as 21 October, 1838.

constituted superior of the Josephites. It was this situation which lay behind the doubt and confusion among the Sisters of the Bathurst diocese.

Even prior to the Sisters' arrival at The Vale, Bishop Matthew Quinn had expressed this opinion.[7] But the founding community at The Vale, and those who later joined them from Adelaide, had received their instruction in the Rule from Mother Mary and Father Woods. They had a clear understanding of the governance of the newly formed Institute. Under the leadership of Sister Teresa, those who joined the Sisters at The Vale had been schooled in their founders' understanding of this aspect of the Rule. Furthermore, Rome had given tacit approval to the Josephite Rule reaffirming and reinforcing the central government of the Institute under a Sister Guardian. In her capacity as the duly elected superior general, Mary MacKillop had visited The Vale and prepared the Sisters to renew their vows according to the newly constituted Rule, which they did in August 1875. The nascent Institute therefore was on a firm canonical footing regarding its government.

Just two months after Mary's visit to The Vale, Bishop Quinn arrived back from Rome. Aware of his desire to assume supreme authority in the Institute, the Sisters grew increasingly anxious. Women, young both in years and religious life and wanting nothing more than to live and work according to the Josephite Rule, they feared what course of action the bishop might take.

It was not until just prior to Christmas that he informed the Sisters of his decision. Those who desired to recognise Mary MacKillop as their superior were to leave the diocese, while those who accepted him as superior of the Sisters in the Bathurst diocese could remain. Though he allowed them complete freedom in the matter, their decisions were not as straightforward and easy as might appear. Of the thirty-six Sisters in the Bathurst diocese, a minority had been appointed to The Vale from Adelaide. Some had been recruited by Quinn from Ireland. Over half were either local women or from some part of the Colony of New South Wales. Of that number some were vowed members of the Institute, while others were still in training. But all were in the Bathurst diocese with the view of living and working in

---

7. Bishop Matthew Quinn to Monsignor Kirby, 18.4.1876. Quinn to Father Julian Tenison Woods, 27.1.1873.

its isolated areas as Sisters of St Joseph. With the bishop's ultimatum, their world was turned up-side-down. For the vast majority of those who had vowed to live according to the Rule which recognised Mary MacKillop as Superior General, the decision was clear-cut. Although it would be difficult, they would leave the diocese. But those still in training—young women away from family and with no other support than that supplied by the Institute—were faced with decisions which would have a bearing on the rest of their lives.

As well as the outward disruption in the lives of the Sisters, there were deeper problems. Under the surface there were rumours about Sisters who might turn against Mary MacKillop, about the future of those in training and about who the bishop might place over them. There was speculation about who might side with Bishop Quinn. Mail was opened, read and information passed on before the letter was finally delivered to the person to whom it was addressed— Mother Mary. There was talk of Sisters' supposed opinions and decisions. Rumours were carried by a Sister to some of the village people. The situation was discussed with at least one of the Bathurst priests. Gossip fuelled the already turbulent situation. The confusion, uncertainty and anxiety experienced by the Sisters could hardly be overestimated.

Amid this state of affairs, Bishop Quinn ordered that the Sisters, who had been on their Christmas holidays at The Vale, were to return to the country convents. Only those who had decided to accept the bishop as superior were to remain at The Vale. He designated the convent at Wattle Flat as the headquarters of those who remained loyal to Mary MacKillop.[8] In doing this, the bishop physically divided the Institute and within weeks the separation was complete with the majority of Sisters going to Adelaide and fourteen remaining at The Vale.[9]

What of Sister Teresa McDonald during this turbulent time? Aware of all that was going on and vitally concerned for her Sisters, the Sister Provincial was unable to take her rightful position in the Institute due

---

8. Wattle Flat is a village situated some 35 kilometres north of Bathurst.
9. For more information on the separation of the Sisters which occurred at The Vale in January and February, 1876, see Marie Crowley, *Women of The Vale: Perthville Josephites 1872–1972* (Richmond, Victoria: Spectrum Publications, 2002), chapter 3.

to the serious deterioration of her health. Too weak and too unwell to take any action, she lay dying. Such was the irony—that one who had so loyally served the Institute both in South Australia and in her first years in the Bathurst diocese should be unable to provide leadership in a time of critical need.

To see Teresa in these last hours of her life allows only a glimpse of a dying woman. To know this Sister whom Mary MacKillop described as 'a priceless treasure,' we must trace her short life back to its beginnings in Scotland.[10] It is to this task that we now turn our attention.

Teresa of the Incarnation

---

10. MacKillop to Woods, 19.9.1872.

2
The Mcdonalds Of Scotland

The Scottish archaeologist, historian, broadcaster and writer, Neil Oliver, makes this observation regarding Scotland and its peoples:

> Scotland is a small country on the edge of Europe, facing west into the harsh Atlantic Ocean. Life has been hard there for most of the people, most of the time. The Industrial Revolution of the eighteenth and nineteenth centuries led to unprecedented population growth, so that a land short of natural resources was soon home to five million people. It was a lot to ask of a nation that had supported rather less than a fifth of that number for almost all of its existence.[1]

He goes on to describe the impact this had on the population:

> A people who had been wanderers by nature became wanderers by necessity. Hundreds of thousands, then millions of Scots found the only solution to problems real or imagined was to leave these shores and make futures in every other corner of the globe. A flow of people that was a trickle in the late seventeenth century became a haemorrhage in the eighteenth, nineteenth and twentieth. . . . For much of her history Scotland has been a home for leaving, in search of dreams.[2]

Among that 'haemorrhage' of people who left home 'in search of dreams' were Martin and Janet McDonald and their five children.

---

1. Neil Oliver, *A History of Scotland* (London: Phoenix, 2009), 433.
2. Neil Oliver, *A History of Scotland*, 433.

The Scottish Highlander, Martin McDonald, was a native of Ardnamurchan. A rugged peninsula which forms the most westerly point of the Scottish mainland, it features in the earliest historical records as a stronghold of various branches of Clan MacDonald. Sources differ as to the date of his birth, but it is thought to be about the year 1818. Janet Young was born in the Lowlands of Scotland in Galston, Ayrshire, situated some thirty-seven kilometres south west of Glasgow. Records indicate that she was born in 1813. Though there are no extant records of their baptisms, the circumstances and events of their later lives confirm that they were baptised in the Catholic Church. Just how the two came to meet remains unknown but at some stage Martin, either as a child with his family or as an adult, moved south from the Highlands to Ayrshire where he met his future wife.

The *Old Parish Registers of the Church of Scotland* record that Martin and Janet were married in Janet's hometown of Galston on 18 March, 1838.[3] The fact that their marriage was recorded in the Register of the Church of Scotland highlights the restrictions under which Scottish Catholics lived from the time of the Reformation into the early nineteenth century. At the time of Martin and Janet's marriage the only legal place for the banns of marriage to be called was the (Presbyterian) Church of Scotland. This meant that sometimes a Catholic marriage could be recorded in the Church of Scotland Old Parish Records while in fact it took place in the presence of a Catholic priest. It also meant that a Catholic marriage could have taken place but was never registered either because records were not kept or had been destroyed due to the laws against Catholics at the time.[4] The details of the McDonald/Young marriage are buried in these confusing and often non-existent records.

---

3. Background information on the McDonald and Young families is minimal and what limited sources are available reveal conflicting places and dates. I am indebted to Mrs Jennie Sach, great grandniece of Margaret (Sister Teresa McDonald), whose research into her family history has provided me with information used in this chapter.

4. The announcement of the banns of marriage in the Church prior to a marriage gave notice to the congregation that a contract of marriage was to take place. A further complication to researching marriage records in Scotland is that their registration became compulsory as late as 1855—seventeen years after the McDonald marriage.

As Oliver wrote regarding Scotland, 'Life has been hard there for most of the people, most of the time.'[5] That would have been the case for Martin and Janet as they grew up. Beginning about the middle of the eighteenth century, the emphasis changed in Scotland from agriculture to industrial development as ships delivered tobacco, sugar and cotton from the Americas and engineering and shipbuilding based on coal, iron and steel quickly developed. An increasing population, boosted by immigration from Ireland, flocked to the Forth and Clyde valleys seeking employment. This combination of industrial and urban expansion resulted in great wealth for some while the majority experienced widespread poverty and deep discrimination. In the cities, where smoke from coal fires hung low, life was fragile and unhygienic. In the Highlands traditional crofts and sometimes entire communities were taken over for the development of large sheep farms.[6] Added to this was the devastation caused by the potato blight of 1846. The dispossessed had to do as best they could which often involved moving to the industrial areas. This situation could well have motivated either the entire McDonald family, or perhaps the young Martin alone, to move south in search of employment. Whatever of that, by early 1838 the 20-year-old had met and married Janet Young, his senior by five years, in Galston. It is impossible to know just to what extent, or if at all, they had been victims of the agricultural, industrial and social upheaval of their country and, as Catholics, suffered from religious discrimination. However, the pattern of their subsequent life in Scotland suggests that they numbered among the poor and knew what it was to struggle for a living.

The newlyweds settled in Galston but it would not be long before a pattern of moving location and changing employment emerged, culminating in the final move to Australia fifteen years later. Those years saw the birth of six children.

Their first child, Margaret (the future Sister Teresa) was born in Janet's hometown, Galston, on 21 October, 1838.[7] The first son of the family, Donald, was born in Erskine located on the southern bank of

---

5. Oliver, *A History of Scotland*, 433.
6. This process became known in history as the Highland Clearances.
7. The date of Margaret's birth is based on that recorded in the Baptismal Register, St John's Church, Portobello, Scotland. It differs from that date given in Crowley, *Women of The Vale*.

the River Clyde, on 29 September, 1840. Baptised within a month of his birth, he died in infancy. By 1841 the family's address was given as Kilmaurs East Side and Martin's occupation as a spirit dealer.[8] It was there that another son, John, was born on 26 November 1841.

It was after John's birth that the decision was made to move to the east coast of Scotland—to the Forth valley. It is possible that Martin sought employment by the North British Railway as the family settled in Markinch, Fife, which was well situated in relation to the developing rail stretching along the east coast of Scotland. It was there that William was born on 19 July, 1843. At some time after that, the family moved south across the Firth of Forth to the coastal town of Musselburgh (Midlothian) near the city of Edinburgh. It is reasonable to conclude that they were settled there by 27 July 1845 for it was on that day that Margaret, John and William were baptised in the Roman Catholic Church of St John the Evangelist, Portobello—now an inner suburb of Edinburgh. At the time Margaret would have been six years old, John four and William nearly two. No extant material provides an explanation for their baptisms at this age, but speculation suggests that there were no Catholic churches or priests in the regions in which the family had previously lived.[9] The fact that the infant Donald was baptised prior to his death indicates that his parents understood and valued the sacrament and that their postponement of the baptism of their other children may have been due to circumstances beyond their control. It was in Musselburgh that the second daughter of the family, Rachel, was born on 26 February, 1847.

The McDonalds' next move was further south to Dalkeith, also in Midlothian. The last son of the family, Donald, was born there on 21 May 1849.[10] By 1851 the family was listed as living at 120 Brewers

---

8. Scotland Census, 1841. This information was provided to me by Sister Philomena Kalmund rsj who accessed it, and a number of other details on the McDonald family, through <www.Ancestry.com.au> Kilmaurs is located some 10 kilometres north east of Galston.

9. It took hundreds of years for the Catholic Church in Scotland to recover from the devastation caused by the Reformation. It is interesting to note that it was not until 1844 that a resident priest was appointed to the parish of St John the Evangelist, Portobello, and that it was only the following year that the three McDonald children, Margaret, John and William, were baptised. <www.stjohnsportobello.co.uk> Accessed 2 October 2015

10. Both Donald and Rachael were baptised in St John the Evangelist, Portobello—Rachel on 21 March, 1847 and Donald on 21 May, 1849. It seems Donald may

Bush and Martin's occupation was given as railway labourer.[11] It is difficult to know exactly where this street, place or road was located. However, being in the civil parish of Cockpen, it was somewhere on the south eastern edge of Edinburgh and close to Dalkeith where Donald was born in 1849. The fact that all their children, except the infant Donald, were baptised in the Catholic Church at Portobello indicates that during the years they lived in Musselburgh, Dalkeith and at 120 Brewers Bush, Martin and Janet recognised this as their parish church. It was while they were living in Brewer's Bush that the last child of the family, Mary, was born on 7 November, 1852. It would be not until a year later, and in a new country, that little Mary would be baptised.[12]

In the early 1850s, the McDonalds of 120 Brewers Bush took stock of their situation. In fifteen years they had lived in five different locations. That constant movement suggests that Martin had difficulty in finding work and in providing a home for his family. He and Janet struggled to keep themselves and their ever increasing family as they moved around Scotland. Part of the vast majority of the poor of their homeland, they looked to the new world 'in search of dreams.'[13] They decided on Australia thus becoming among the ninety thousand Scots who emigrated to Australia in the early 1850s.[14] Martin, the railway labourer, put forward his occupation as 'shepherd and ploughman,' possibly so he would be favoured by the Emigration Commissioners

---

have been called after his brother who died in 1840, but there is some conjecture that the son born in 1849 may have been not Donald, but Daniel.

11. Scotland Census, 1851. The Census confirms that Brewers Bush (a Street, Place or Road) was located in the civil parish of Cockpen. This civil parish was located in the east of Edinburghshire containing at its south west corner the village of Bonnyrigg (located 2 miles from Dalkeith which was not located in the civil parish of Cockpen) and a number of other villages and hamlets. See Frances Groome, *Ordinance Gazetteer of Scotland 1882–1884* at <www.visionofbritain. org.uk/place/16675> Accessed 10 October 2015.

12. Baptismal Register of the Archives of the Roman Catholic Archdiocese of Perth. My special thanks goes to the archivist, Stefania Di Maria, who persevered in the search for this record.

13. Oliver, *A History of Scotland*, 433.

14. Thomas Devine, *The Scottish Nation 1700–2007* (London, Penguin, 2006), 470–471.

who looked for men who could contribute to the developing wool and wheat industry of the Swan River Settlement.[15]

Thus it was that Martin and Janet together with their six children, Margaret, John, William, Rachel, Donald and three months old Mary packed their few belongings and farewelled family and friends. No doubt they carried with them the memory of their first son and brother who lay buried in Erskine. The family arrived at the port of Liverpool, England, in March, 1853. Emigrants under the authority of the Colonial Land and Emigration Commissioners, they boarded the ship *Sabrina* bound for Western Australia. With two hundred and twenty-nine passengers on board, it sailed from Liverpool on 13 March 1853. After a voyage of ninety-one days, it arrived at its destination on 13 June.

Teresa of the Incarnate

---

15. Crew and Passenger List for the *Sabrina*. Western Australia Crew and Passenger Lists 1852 –1930. <www.Ancestry.com.au> Accessed 15 October 2015.

3
The Mcdonalds Of Western Australia

Although the Swan River Colony was settled by Europeans as 'free' in 1829, within 20 years it became obvious that the lack of a workforce was hampering its development. In order to remedy that situation, the authorities decided to import cheap convict labour to assist in the construction of public works. The first convict transport sailed into the Port of Fremantle in 1850. One section of the newly arrived labour force was sent to the recently established village of Guildford where a convict depot was established.[1]

Martin McDonald's plan of getting employment in the developing pastoral or agricultural industry of the Colony proved difficult to achieve. However, the large number of convict gangs involved in a variety of public works required overseers and Martin soon realised it was there that he would get work. When he applied for employment to the Comptroller General of Convicts he was taken on as an Assistant Overseer of Convicts at the convict depot at Guildford. By early August 1853 he was overseeing a road gang working in the area.[2] It was in a private home in Guildford that the baby Mary, born prior to the family's departure from Scotland, was baptised on 6 November 1853.[3] The following year the McDonalds were registered

---

1. Guildford, originally a market town and inland port located on the Swan River, was one of the first European settlements in the Swan River Colony. Situated some twelve kilometres northeast of Perth CBD, today it is a thriving suburb listed on the National Trust Register.
2. David Barker, (compiler), *Warders and Gaolers: A Dictionary of Western Australian Prison Officers 1829–1879* Perth: Western Australian Genealogical Society, 2000), 117.
3. Baptism Register of the Roman Catholic Archdiocese of Perth. Mary was baptised by Father Raphael Martelli and her godparents were Margaret McDonald and James Lloyd.

as occupying a Guildford Town Lot.[4] It was also in 1854 that Bishop Salvado included Martin and Janet McDonald and their children on the list of Roman Catholics living in the diocese of Perth.[5]

These facts confirm that after his arrival in Australia Martin McDonald lost no time in securing employment or in providing a home for his family. Martin had, however, a checkered career during the nearly two years that he worked with the convicts. The first appraisal (19 November 1853) of his overseeing earned commendation from the Comptroller General: 'A zealous and most useful officer and very under paid.'[6] A later report (26 July 1854) notes that 'as regards his charge of works he always gave satisfaction.' But this was not always the case. At Guildford he was found guilty (3 July 1854) of 'breach of trust,' of being 'unfit to be trusted with charge of a detached party' and of neglecting to give appropriate directions to the convicts. On another occasion (21 July 1854) he was charged with having directed convicts to carry out private work on the family home, but he was later exonerated.[7] Late in 1854 he was charged with stealing an amount of bread. At times reduced in rank for a period of time, fined some weeks' pay and even dismissed but subsequently reinstated, Martin was finally dismissed on 30 June 1855 because 'he [was] supernumerary and his services [were] no longer required.'

Given his record of employment in Scotland and in the Swan River Settlement, the conclusion could be drawn that Martin was of unreliable character. But the McDonalds had left Scotland and arrived in Australia a poor family. One report from his employees in Guildford notes that Martin was 'very under paid.' There is little doubt that he struggled to keep his wife and six children. A man forced into that position had few alternatives. Whatever the reasons behind Martin's unstable employment record and final dismissal, the consequences were formidable. The McDonalds struggled to exist.

It was during these years at Guildford that Margaret McDonald grew to adulthood. Whether she attended school after her arrival in

---

4. *The Bicentennial Dictionary of Western Australians 1829–1888* (Perth: University of Western Australia Press, 1988), 1961.

5. *The Bicentennial Dictionary of Western Australians 1829–1888* (Perth: University of Western Australia Press, 1988), 1961.

6. This and all the following reports regarding Martin's employment as an Overseer of Convicts are taken from Barker, *Warders and Gaolers*, 117.

7. He was exonerated on the evidence of the Senior Assistant Superintendent at Guildford who had given his approval for the convicts to do this work on a Good Friday holiday.

Australia is unknown. Given the custom and necessity of the time, it is highly probable that she was fully occupied helping her mother with the cooking, running the house and caring for the younger members of the family especially the baby, Mary. Though a young woman living in an isolated area of a region only recently settled by Europeans, her experiences of life ran deep. From Scotland she had carried the memories of the poverty of the majority of the population, of constantly moving as her father sought and found work. Then at Guildford she saw the convicts at work, experienced her father's apparent instability and shared her mother's constant struggle to feed the family. It was during those formative years that the qualities which later caused Mary MacKillop to describe Margaret as 'a priceless treasure' had their beginnings.[8]

There is no extant record of Martin's subsequent employment in the Swan River Settlement. That the family remained in that Colony for another year and a half after his dismissal by the Comptroller General of Convicts confirms that he did find work. But things had not gone well for the McDonalds during their first years in Australia. There remains no written evidence as to why Martin and Janet began to look further afield. One reason could have been that Martin sought to move away from the harsh environment of dealing with convicts. They had saved enough money to make a new start. Their choice was South Australia.

A little more than three and a half years after the McDonalds had sailed into Fremantle harbour on board the *Sabrina*, they assembled on the same wharf to board the *New Perseverance* bound for Port Adelaide on her maiden voyage.[9] No doubt they were continuing 'in search of dreams.'[10] They were not to know that the next thirty-six days would see the near shattering of those dreams.

Upon boarding the *New Perseverance* they found the passengers to be mostly time-expired convicts and military pensioners.[11] Among

---

8. MacKillop to Father Tenison Woods, 19.9.1871.
9. The *New Perseverance* was a two-masted schooner 84.8 x 20.7 x 10.2 feet in dimensions and weighing 105 tons, built and owned by time-expired convict, Sam Breakes. Rod Dickson, (translated and compiled), *Ships Registered in Western Australia from 1856 to 1969 Their Details, Owners and Their Fate*, published privately, 1956. <www.maritimeheritage.org.au> Accessed 17 October 2015.
10. Oliver, *A History of Scotland*, 433.
11. The British government sometimes employed retired military men to guard

the others sailing to Port Adelaide were two young Dubliners, Christopher Reynolds and Frederick Byrne. Former members of the Benedictine Order in Perth, they were to resume their studies for the priesthood at Sevenhill and after ordination take up ministry in the diocese of Adelaide.[12] The McDonalds and the seminarians soon struck up a friendship. On 25 January 1857 with all forty-seven passengers on board, the *New Perseverance* weighed anchor.[13] Before she could set sail the vessel was boarded by police. They ordered the anchor to be let down, found many stolen items on board and arrested both the owner and the captain who were committed for trial the following day. Anxious to get the voyage underway, the authorities employed a ticket-of-leave man as captain as well as a policeman to be his guardian. Captain Adams finally weighed anchor on 28 January by which time, unbeknown to the authorities, much of the food and other provisions had been stolen.

No sooner was the voyage underway than misfortune struck.

> The top spars gave way at the first strain, in consequence of which the schooner could carry only the main and fore sails, which having been saturated with salt water and exposed to the sun, were rotten and required constant mending and patching. The joinings of her timbers were so badly caulked that she took in a great deal of water, which required a pump to be worked night and day.[14]

Irrespective of these difficulties, the vessel reached within about ninety miles off Kangaroo Island where it was becalmed. More trouble followed. Captain Adams became so ill he was unable to leave his cabin. The repercussions of the stolen food emerged when the steward reported that supplies were reduced to one bag of biscuits among the forty-seven passengers plus crew. At the captain's direction, these biscuits were divided among everyone on board—three per

---

the convicts on their voyage from England to the Swan River Settlement. These pensioners were allowed to bring their families and then settle in the Colony but were free to move to other colonies if they chose.

12. Both men were ordained in 1860. Reynolds was ordained bishop of the diocese of Adelaide in 1873 and figured significantly in the history of Mary MacKillop and the Sisters of St Joseph.

13. The eye witness account of this voyage is taken from Frederick Byrne, *History of the Catholic Church in South Australia* (Adelaide: J P Hansen, 1914), 88–94.

14. Byrne, *History of the Catholic Church in South Australia*, 90. ASSJA.

person for the first three days and then two per day for the next three days. The situation became grave. On the evening of the sixth day, a westerly wind sprang up and drove the schooner into Spencers Gulf. The following morning a ship, the *Ascendent* from London, was seen astern. After messages were sent and the chief officer of the *Ascendent* saw for himself the desperate state of the passengers and crew of the *New Perseverance*, food and medicines were delivered to the stricken schooner. With this assistance those on board were able to survive until the *New Perseverance* reached Port Adelaide on 6 March 1857. The voyage from Fremantle to Adelaide had taken thirty-six days.

The frightening experience of this journey must have made a significant impact on the 17-year-old Margaret McDonald. Though there are no extant records in which she recounted or commented on those 36 days, Christopher Reynolds, who remained a firm friend of the family, wrote of her later as his 'old shipmate'.[15]

The family settled into their new life. Martin quickly found employment with the Adelaide Municipal Corporation as a labourer and later as a stationman. Records indicate that this involved road work and later supervision of road workers under the authority of the city surveyor. Martin brought with him his experience in building and maintaining roads, although in South Australia he was working not with convicts but with a free labour force. By 1866 he had been given additional duties as an inspector for the Municipal Corporation.[16] That he did well from the time of his arrival in Adelaide is evidenced by the fact that towards the end of 1860 he had purchased a portion of land and a house 'being part of the Town Acre numbered 191' in Weymouth Street.[17] In 1864 his property consisted of a house and shop on the corner of Weymouth and Crowther Streets. Two years later

---

15. Sister Calasanctius Howley wrote that when we told the Bishop [Reynolds] that Sister [Teresa] was dead, he seemed to feel it so much. He said, 'Poor Teresa, my old shipmate, so you are gone before me.' Howley to MacKillop, 12.1.1876.
16. In a meeting of the Adelaide Municipal Council (5 March 1866) a letter from Martin McDonald was tabled seeking an increase in pay of 6d per day. The request was granted on the grounds that he had extra work as an inspector. *South Australian Weekly Chronicle*, 16 March 1866. <www.trove.nla.gov.au/ndp/del/article94741678> Accessed 17 October 2015.
17. Certificate of Title, Register Book vol. xvii, folio 18, 21 March, 1860; Letters from Adelaide Council to Martin McDonald 8 October, 1861, 19 August 1862, 10 July 1865. Letters from Martin McDonald to Adelaide Council 21 January 1869, 21 January 1869, 12 March 1870. I gratefully acknowledge the research and contribution of Mrs Jennie Sach who obtained copies of the original Certificate of Title and letters from Adelaide City Council Report.

an area of vacant land adjacent to the shop was purchased. Extensive research has failed to identify the nature of the shop. Martin referred to it as 'my store' which might suggest it supplied haberdashery, small goods and/or clothes.[18] Years later when Margaret (Sister Teresa) was stationed in Penola she told Mary MacKillop that she had asked Rachel (presumably her sister Rachel McDonald) to send some materials and wool from Adelaide. This might indicate that Rachel continued to run the shop which their father had established.[19]

When the McDonalds arrived in Adelaide John, at fifteen was a young man. William was thirteen, Rachel nine and Donald seven. The baby of the family, Mary, would turn five at the end of the year. Their father was approaching forty years of age, while their mother was moving into her middle forties. Adelaide became their home as the members of the family matured and established lives of their own. In later years, Martin and Janet moved to Kulpara, South Australia, where Janet died in 1882 and Martin in 1892.[20] They are both buried in the Kulpara cemetery.[21]

It is here that we leave the family as we take up the story of Margaret, the future Sister Teresa.

18. City of Adelaide *Rate Assessment Book* 1847–1870. I gratefully acknowledge the assistance given by Rod Thornton, Snr Archivist, Adelaide City Council. <www.photosau.com.au/adelaiderates/scripts/home.asp> Accessed 12 November 2015 Martin McDonald to His Worship the Mayor and Councillors of the City of Adelaide, 12 March 1870.
19. McDonald to MacKillop, 15.5.1868; 16.10.1868.
20. Janet McDonald and Martin McDonald in the Australian Death Index, 178 –1985. <www.search.ancestry.com.au> Accessed 12 November 2015.
21. Though both Martin and Janet are recorded as buried in the Old Portion of the Kulpara cemetery, the location of their graves is unknown. *Book of Burials in Kulpara Cemetery*, Adelaide City Council.

4
Ten Years In Adelaide

When Margaret McDonald stepped onto the wharf at Port Adelaide in March 1857, she was a young woman of 18. The daunting journey to Adelaide was at an end and life in new surroundings lay before her. About the same time, another harrowing journey was being endured and a destination finally reached. The 24-year-old priest, Julian Tenison Woods was about to board the steamer, *Boomerang*, on the short voyage from Adelaide to Robe. By strange coincidence it too became becalmed off Kangaroo Island and food ran scarce. By the time Julian finally reached his new parish, Penola, it was the middle of March, 1857. He too was on the threshold of an unknown future. And in faraway Melbourne preparations were being made for yet another journey. Later in 1857, the MacKillop family was to move to Sydney and with them would be Mary who, at fifteen years of age, was the eldest. The sojourn in Sydney would be short. The return voyage as steerage passengers in the coastal steamer, made only after Mary's mother borrowed money for the fares, was to be overshadowed by worry about the future. As the boat steamed into Port Philip Bay, Mary had no idea what the years ahead would hold. For all three—Margaret, Julian and Mary then unknown to each other—1857 was a year of arriving at journey's end with an unknown future stretching before them. Yet Providence was to draw them into a shared future in the most unexpected way.

It would not be until six days prior to her 29th birthday that Margaret's future would finally be settled. While there are no extant

records of how she actually spent those intervening 10 years, there are some clues which throw light on her life during that time.[1]

As she had done in Guildford, Margaret would have continued to assist her mother with the many household tasks of a big family. No doubt the McDonalds quickly sought out the Catholic church and began to attend Mass and to participate in parish activities. It was there that Margaret met Miss Ellen McMullen, a teacher in charge of a private school, who helped out in the parish by attending to the sanctuary lamp in the Cathedral.[2] She had emigrated from Ireland and though the year of her arrival in Adelaide is uncertain, there are indications that she was there by 1858. Margaret, the young woman from Scotland and the Irish teacher, Ellen, developed a firm friendship. In 1863 Ellen moved to Melbourne where she spent eighteen months as a postulant and novice with the Sisters of Mercy but when that did not work out, she returned to Adelaide and to teaching.[3] Their friendship continued and later events suggest that Margaret could well have assisted Ellen in caring for the cathedral and in her work in the classroom.[4]

As mentioned in the previous chapter, by 1864 Martin McDonald's property was described as a house and shop and he referred to the shop as 'my store.' At that time Martin was still employed by the Adelaide Municipal Council, so he would not have had the time to manage and operate the store. The description given of the house and shop indicate they were the one building—a convenient situation for both running the family home and attending to customers. It seems reasonable to suppose that Margaret and her mother filled both these roles.

1.   That there are no extant records of her life in Scotland, Guildford or Adelaide left by Margaret could be due to her observance of Father Tenison Woods' direction to the Sisters: 'Let us never speak of our friends or homes, as this leads to much distraction and excites vanity and jealousy.' Father Julian Tenison Woods, *Explanation of the Rule and Constitution of the Sisters of St Joseph*, chapter 7.

2.   A Sister of St Joseph, *Life of Mother Mary Foundress of the Sisterhood of St Joseph of the Sacred Heart* (Westmead, Sydney: Sisters of St Joseph, 1916), 12.

3.   Information supplied by Marie Therese Foale rsj.

4.   After Margaret's (Sister Teresa McDonald's) death in 1876, Ellen (Sister Josephine McMullen) referred to the long years she had known her. McMullen to MacKillop January, 1876. Another wrote of the effect of the death: 'Poor Sister Josephine felt it very much. You know they were old friends.' Sister Joseph to MacKillop, January, 1876.

There can be no doubt that during her ten years in Adelaide and through her association with Ellen McMullen, Margaret reflected upon the direction of her own life. It would have been a significant move for Ellen to go to Melbourne and join the Sisters of Mercy and then to return to Adelaide. The two women would have discussed this and, as later events show, Margaret herself had begun to feel drawn to the religious life. But there were the responsibilities of her family and the shop. As there were no congregations of religious women in Adelaide at that time, joining one must have seemed a distant dream to Margaret.

It was towards the end of her 10 years in Adelaide that events in the south of the Colony and the diocese began to take a direction that would have a bearing on Margaret's life. Just as 1857 had seen a journey's end for Margaret McDonald, Mary McKillop and Father Tenison Woods, so 1867 would signal another journey's end for the two women and the priest.

In the early 1860s Mary MacKillop moved from Melbourne to take up a position as governess to her cousins on a station near Penola in South Australia. There she met Father Tenison Woods who had been appointed to the Penola parish three years prior to her arrival. It was also about that time that the newly appointed bishop of Adelaide, Patrick Bonaventure Geoghegan, issued a *Pastoral Letter* in which he implored the priests of his diocese to establish independent Catholic schools for all Catholic children. Father Woods took the bishop's orders very seriously. By way of response, he determined to establish a new religious order for women who would be prepared to live in the harsh conditions of the isolated areas of the Colony. Mary MacKillop, who had experienced a longing to serve God in the religious life, responded to Woods' idea. Towards the end of 1865 she began teaching in the Catholic school at Penola and on 19 March 1866 adopted a simple rule of life as devised by Woods. The new religious order was underway.

One year after the foundation of the Sisters of St Joseph in Penola, Father Woods left his parish for a new appointment as Director of Education in Adelaide. While it seems likely that both Margaret McDonald and Ellen McMullen knew of the developments in Penola before Woods returned to Adelaide, he certainly told them about the new Institute after his arrival. Because it had been decided that

Sister Mary MacKillop and a Sister companion would also move to Adelaide, Woods was looking for a suitable house as their convent. In this task he sought the help of Ellen who arranged accommodation for them in a house in Grote Street. Within days she joined the new Institute taking the name Josephine.[5] Later in the year (on 15 October 1867), Margaret also joined the Sisters of St Joseph taking the name Sister Teresa of the Incarnation. It was the feast day of her namesake St Teresa who, in 1536, entered the Carmelite Convent of the Incarnation in Avila, Spain.

The year of 1867 brought Margaret McDonald, Mary MacKillop and Father Woods to the end of another journey. Mary and Woods had travelled from Penola to Adelaide. Though the future of their lives or of the new Institute was not clear, they trusted that God would show them the way. Margaret had travelled from Weymouth to Grote Street—geographically a short distance but inwardly a deep wrench. She too was unaware of what lay ahead and trusted in God. As Sister Teresa of the Incarnation she was setting out on a new journey.

---

5. Sister Josephine McMullen's sense of the early Josephite spirit, teaching ability, maturity and integrity contributed to the strength and stability of the Institute during its early years and in several demanding situations. She died in North Sydney in 1904.

5
Teresa And The Sisters Of St Joseph

Although the diocese of Adelaide had been established in 1842, the Catholic Church throughout the Colony was still in its early stages of development when Teresa joined the Josephites. The colonial population was strongly Protestant. The small minority of Catholics were mostly of Irish descent, poor and unable to provide much financial support for the diocese. The first bishop, Francis Murphy, had died a year after the McDonald family's arrival in Adelaide in 1857. Patrick Bonaventure Geoghegan who succeeded him had died in Ireland before taking over his new appointment as bishop of the diocese of Goulburn. A year prior to Teresa's arrival at the Grote Street convent in 1867, the Irish Franciscan Lawrence Bonaventure Sheil had been installed as bishop of Adelaide, a position he would hold until his death in 1872.

Though the poverty of the diocese in its early years was slightly alleviated by the granting of government funds to religion and education, Catholics were dealt a severe blow when those funds were halted by the Education Act of 1851. Henceforward State aid to religion was abolished and schools were placed under the control of the State in such a way that instruction in any particular denomination was forbidden. Only a few Catholic schools survived—largely through circumvention of the new laws. But Bishop Geoghegan's *Pastoral Letter* stirred the priests and parents into action so that by August 1866 there were twenty-three independent Catholic schools located in various parts of the diocese.[1] Short on funds, often lacking

---

1. Marie Therese Foale, *The Josephite Story: The Sisters of St Joseph: their foundation and early history 1866–1893* (Sydney: St Joseph's Generalate, 1989), 8. For a full account of the early history of the Catholic Church in South Australia see

properly qualified teachers, operating in substandard buildings with inadequate equipment, and devoid of a defined education policy on which to base their existence or future, these schools struggled.

Such was the situation of education within the diocese when, in September 1866, Bishop Sheil appointed Father Tenison Woods Director General of Catholic Education, Chairman of the Board and Inspector of Schools throughout the diocese.[2] In addition, Woods was also to serve as the bishop's secretary. It was clear that the new Director was faced with an enormous task in regard to the schools. He soon became aware of other urgent needs in Adelaide. Unemployed single girls who had migrated to the Colony were at moral risk and newly released prisoners lacked shelter and employment. Many babies and children were in need of a safe place where they would receive care. The Director of Education saw an answer to the urgency of these demands in Mary MacKillop and her companions who had recently opened a house in Adelaide. It was against this background of need throughout the diocese and in Adelaide that Sister Teresa had left her home and her family to join the band of women whose primary ministry was education but who would serve also wherever there was a need of any kind.

When Teresa arrived at the small Grote Street convent she joined a small group of women still in religious formation. The first Josephite community in Australia, they had much to learn. The ink on the *Rules of The Institute of St Joseph for the Catholic Education of Poor Children* written by Father Woods for this Australian religious Institute was hardly dry as they gathered around the Father Founder. He provided them with personal spiritual direction and instruction in the foundational tenets of religious life and in the particular character and spirit of the newly written Rule. Sharing day-to-day life with Mary MacKillop was in itself a rich lesson. As co-founders, Mary and Father Woods shared the dreams, hopes and plans for the Institute. By the time of her arrival in Adelaide therefore, Mary, though herself new in religious life, was able to give some guidance in the meaning of the Josephite Rule and in the practical aspects of actually living it.

Margaret Press, *From our Broken Toil: South Australian Catholics 1836–1906* (Adelaide: Catholic Archdiocese of Adelaide, 1986) and Foale, *The Josephite Story.*

2. Woods to MacKillop 19.9.1866.

It was in this environment enriched by the presence and instruction of both Father Woods and Mother Mary that Teresa took her first steps in religious life as a Sister of St Joseph.

The first stage of training for religious life is the postulancy. That is followed by the postulant's formal entry into the novitiate when she is 'received' and referred to as a 'novice.' At the conclusion of the novitiate the novice, if she so desires and is considered by her superiors to be suitable for religious life, takes vows. For the Sisters of St Joseph, these were the three vows of poverty, chastity and obedience. During the early years of the Institute, a fourth vow to promote the love of Jesus Christ in the hearts of little children was added. In the established Congregations of European origin these stages of training spanned specific time periods and later, when their Rule became established, it was the same for the Sisters of St Joseph. But in their early years, when the Josephites first gathered as a religious Institute still very much in the making, such organised periods of training were not observed. Nor had the position of Sister Guardian General, referred to in the original Rule, been officially recognised.[3] To all intents and purposes Father Woods, referred to as 'Father Director', was the superior of the Institute. In his role of Director General of Catholic Education he was acutely aware of the urgent need for Sisters in the schools. He saw no other option than to bypass their training to a large extent and appoint them to existing or new Catholic schools.

Thus it was that, immediately upon her entry into the Institute, Teresa began teaching at St Francis Xavier's Cathedral Hall School located in Wakefield Street. Shortly after their arrival in Adelaide, the Sisters had taken charge of this school. Mary MacKillop, with her assistants Sister Rose Cunningham and the postulant Ellen McMullen, set about organising it according to the time-table, rules and curriculum which she had formulated and practised in Penola. As we saw earlier, Teresa, prior to her joining the Josephites, could well have had teaching experience in the private Catholic school run by Ellen McMullen in the Cathedral Hall. Whatever of that, at the Hall School she was trained in the methods devised by Mary MacKillop.

---

3. The first Rule for the Sisters of St Joseph was written by Father Woods early in 1867. On 17 December 1868 Bishop Sheil approved that Rule, officially named *Rules of the Institute of St Joseph for the Catholic Education of Poor Children*, for the use of the Sisters of St Joseph in the diocese of Adelaide.

It was this system she would establish and maintain in the schools where she taught.

But Teresa did not remain for long at the Hall School. Prior to her joining the group in Grote Street, Father Woods had appointed two Sisters from that community to take charge of the Catholic school at Bowden—located some three kilometres from the city. By early November 1867, just a few weeks after her arrival at Grote Street, Teresa was also appointed to the Bowden school. The fact that she continued to live with the Grote Street community meant that she could still receive the training in religious life given by Father Woods and Mary MacKillop.[4]

Although the co-founders had planned that all postulants would have to work in the schools for three months before being received into the Grote Street convent, this was not the case for Teresa or for many of the first women to join the Institute.[5] On 21 November 1867, some five weeks after she had begun her postulancy, Teresa was received formally as a novice and named in the Institute Register as the eighth woman to enter the Sisters of St Joseph. With this, she laid aside the black dress which had distinguished her as a postulant and in a simple ceremony donned the habit and veil of the Josephites.

When the year 1867 concluded, membership of the Institute had risen to ten and the schools closed for the Christmas holidays.[6] All the members of the Josephite community met at Grote Street to celebrate Christmas, to participate in a retreat and to enjoy a short break together. It was also at that time that the first Chapter or formal meeting was held during which Father Woods named Sister Mary as Little Sister (that is the name for Superioress).[7] Sisters Clare Wright (Little Sister), Teresa McDonald and Gertrude Hayman were appointed to open the first Josephite convent at the copper mining town of Kapunda situated about eighty-two kilometres north-east of Adelaide. On 12 January 1868 they set out for their new home.[8]

---

4. Sister Clare Wright to MacKillop and Rose Cunningham, 6.11.1867. Foale, *The Josephite Story*, 42.
5. Woods to MacKillop, 28.5.1867.
6. Register of the Sisters of St Joseph.
7. Woods to Miss Phillips, 7.2.1868.
8. The eight day retreat was conducted by Father Polk SJ. Woods to Miss Anna Phillips, 7.2.1868. It is assumed that the Sisters travelled by train, the line between Adelaide and Kapunda having been opened in 1860.

On arrival at Kapunda the community soon settled into their new home. For the first time Teresa had the experience of living and working in a country convent. The community was an interesting mix. At twenty-nine years of age, Teresa was the eldest and a Scot. Clare, just twenty-four was born in Portland, Victoria. The twenty-one-year old Gertrude was English. Teresa and Clare were novices and Gertrude a postulant. Clare had joined the Grote Street community just a few months before Teresa. Having opened the Institute's first branch house at Yankalilla in 1867, she had some experience of setting up a foundation of Josephite life in a country town. Gertrude had been with the Sisters for just five weeks.[9] Anxious to begin well among people who had no experience of the newly-founded Australian Religious Institute, they faced the demands of successfully establishing themselves in the existing school and faithfully living the Josephite Rule. This required hard work and long hours especially for women who were new and inexperienced in their work and their way of life. Mary MacKillop, who may have accompanied them to Kapunda and helped them settle in, certainly visited soon after their arrival. Classes began in the church on 20 January with 100 pupils. By the end of the year the numbers had almost doubled and Sister Clare was able to report that the Vicar General, who visited the school, was 'very pleased' with the children.[10] In addition, the Sisters had begun catechism classes each Sunday at Johnstown, later called St John's, a settlement located about five kilometres southeast of Kapunda. So pleased were the people to have this instruction for their children that they took turns to collect the Sisters from the convent each week and return them.[11] But, as Teresa wrote to Father Woods: 'There is a great deal to be done in Kapunda. The people are very careless about their duty.'[12]

As the summer of 1868 wore on, the heat, the demands of the school and the rigour of religious life soon began to take their toll. It seems too that excessive earnestness and inexperience in the religious life may have contributed to the difficulties the community

---

9. Register of the Sisters of St Joseph.
10. Diary of the Sisters of St Joseph, Kapunda, 1868. Wright to MacKillop, 15.2.1868.
11. Wright to MacKillop, 15.2.1868.
12. McDonald to Woods, 9.3.1868. 'Duty' refers to the obligation to attend Mass, receive Holy Communion and go to the sacrament of Penance.

experienced. It was Teresa who took the initiative in this situation by writing of her concern to Father Woods:

> I intended to write on Saturday, thinking it my duty to tell you about my Sisters who are fasting and I think they are not able to do so, especially in this hot weather. Indeed, if anyone ought to fast, it ought to be me and so I can, but I cannot look at others doing so without speaking about it. They are both ill. Sister Clare has a cold and sore throat and loses her voice. Sister Gertrude has the face-ache, and they feel the heat very much. Please God, the weather will soon change and then we will be all right again.[13]

Then she added something about herself. 'I recommend myself most earnestly to your prayers. I am weary of myself and everyone else.' Clare assured Father Woods that it was not fasting but the heat that exhausted her. She continued: 'I intended to have written a long letter to you, but have not time and do not feel able . . . I sometimes wonder that I have been able to keep up all day, but our B. Lord gives me strength to do a little for him.'[14]

But Clare's illness proved to be more serious than heat exhaustion. A week after her letter to Father Woods, Teresa was reporting to Mary MacKillop that Clare 'is better, thank God, but is still weak. The doctor says there is now no danger. We were very anxious and felt a little lonely.' Teresa herself was also experiencing difficulties which she mentioned to Mary: 'I have had to give up study for some time, my eyes being sore.'[15] This was to be a worsening condition until the end of her life.

We do not know the exact nature of the fast the Sisters were keeping but given the time of the year, we can surmise that it was the Lenten fast. Church law for adults at that time prescribed restrictions on the amount of food eaten during Lent. The Sisters would have been most diligent in keeping the Lenten fast. Clare and Teresa had been with the Institute for less than a year and what little instruction they had from the co-founders had taken place in between teaching. Gertrude's training would have been negligible. Far removed from the

---

13. McDonald to Woods, 9.3.1868
14. She wrote this note on the back of the page of Teresa's letter.
15. McDonald to MacKillop, 16.3.1868.

Grote Street Sisters and very much dependent on their own resources, the Kapunda community had only the Rule to guide their living of the religious life. The Josephite Rule included regulations regarding fasting.[16] In addition, a constant theme of the Rule was mortification, renunciation and the acceptance of difficulties as crosses enabling union with a crucified Christ. Committed to keeping every Church law, and to faithfully living the spirit of the Rule, the inexperienced Sisters—sick and exhausted—laboured in the heat of Kapunda.

It is this unfortunate experience which provides a glimpse into the character of Teresa McDonald. It was she who recognised the imprudence of the situation. Though she was not the Little Sister, she was not afraid to put it honestly and bluntly to Woods: 'they are not able to do so,' 'they are both ill,' 'I cannot look at others doing so without speaking about it.' She did not hesitate to speak about herself: 'I am weary of myself and everyone else.'[17] Her sound judgement came to the fore in her own struggle and that of her and her Sisters. Underlying Teresa's prudent, sensible and down-to-earth attitude was a tender-heartedness and kindness founded in love and compassion. While in later years her prudence was to be sorely tested, her deep love and compassion were to remain a hallmark of her life.

The year of 1868 saw a dramatic increase in numbers in the Institute. By Christmas of that year fifty Sisters of St Joseph, the vast majority still in training, were either teaching or running homes or shelters for those in need. One of these, St Joseph's Refuge, began in Franklin Street but relocated to Mitcham in 1870. Later it was to become significant in Teresa's story. In the meantime the increase in numbers had necessitated a move to a larger house in Adelaide. At first the Sisters occupied some cottages in Franklin Street and later rented a house in Gouger Street. By June 1869 they had moved to another location in Franklin Street to which a chapel was added in 1871. It was here that Teresa was to later witness momentous happenings in Josephite history and to demonstrate her unswerving loyalty to Mary MacKillop.

---

16. The Rule of the Sisters of St Joseph directed that 'Meat will be allowed on all days except the fasts of the Church and Wednesdays and Saturdays; the former in honour of St Joseph; the latter in honour of the glorious Mother of God.'

17. Unfortunately Woods' reply to Teresa's letter is not extant. Neither is any reference by Mary MacKillop to that particular situation in Kapunda.

One of the characteristics of the early years of the Josephite Institute was the frequent movement of Sisters between convents, schools and towns. This was necessary because of the rapid increase in the number of schools they staffed, the requirement that there be at least one experienced teacher in each school, and sometimes because of illness or difficulties in school or community. Sister Teresa was not to escape this situation. In April 1868, a little more than a month after her letter to Father Woods, she received word of her appointment to Penola as Little Sister of the community and in charge of the school. Her companion was to be the 16-year-old old Sister Agnes Smith who had joined the Institute on 4 April of that year and had been received into the novitiate only weeks afterwards.

Teresa of the Incarnat.

6
Penola

When Mary MacKillop and Rose Cunningham left Penola in June 1867 to establish the Institute in Adelaide, Annie MacKillop had been left to run the Penola school.[1] Now less than a year later, Teresa began preparations to travel to the small town where the Institute had its beginnings. Even by today's standards, it was a long journey.

First, she made the train journey to Adelaide. For one who only a few weeks before had spoken of the loneliness of the Kapunda community, it was a delight to be united with Mary MacKillop and the other Adelaide Sisters. Awaiting her also was the other member of the future Penola community. Elizabeth Smith had joined the Institute on 4 April 1868 taking the name Agnes. Of Irish birth, she was sixteen years of age. She was greatly surprised when, at eleven o'clock on the morning of Monday 27 April, Father Woods announced that he would formally receive her into the Institute. There was a flurry to find the necessary habit and veil but all was ready for Father Woods to perform the simple ceremony at midday of the same day. Teresa and Agnes then hurried to gather their few belongings ready to leave for Penola that afternoon. They were accompanied by Mary MacKillop who would help them in setting up the convent and settling into the school.

---

1. Annie was Mary MacKillop's sister. Julia Fitzgerald had come to Australia from Ireland with her parents who settled in Sydney. After her mother's death in 1842 and her father's remarriage in 1844, Julia, with some members of the family moved to Portland in Western Victoria. It was there or on her brother's property near Harrow, also in Western Victoria, that Julia first met Father Woods and Mary MacKillop. She joined the Institute in October 1867. Information supplied by Marie Therese Foale rsj.

Teresa had much to think about on the journey. It had been just over six months since she joined the Institute. Her teaching experience prior to her entry, together with that gained at the Hall school, Bowden and Kapunda stood her in good stead for her charge of the Penola school. Her sound judgement and down-to-earth attitude had come to the fore in the Kapunda community. But for all that and irrespective of her deep faith and resolve, she had received little training in the religious life. The other community member, Agnes, had no training as a teacher or as a religious so would require as much assistance as Teresa had time to provide. Indeed, the two novices had little more to guide them than the Josephite Rule. In appointing Teresa to Penola, Father Woods and Sister Mary had asked a great deal of the wise and compassionate Scot.

The new arrivals lost no time in settling into the rooms at the back of the schoolhouse and into their new assignment. In this they were assisted by Mary MacKillop, who in returning to Penola was reunited with some of her family and back to the scene of the beginnings of the Institute. Then, on Monday 4 May, just a week after their arrival, Teresa and Agnes began teaching the thirty-seven children named on the roll at St Joseph's School.[2] The pupils were a pleasant surprise. Agnes was 'astonished' at their good behaviour and reported back to Adelaide that 'even the little ones were so good.'[3] Soon Mary was on her way back to Grote Street and Teresa took on the full responsibility of both convent and school.[4]

One great advantage that Teresa had at Penola was that she was taking over a well-established school. The stable in which Mary MacKillop had begun classes had been renovated by her brother John so when Teresa and Agnes arrived it was a presentable schoolroom. An even greater advantage was that the Syllabus for Each Class, Programme of Lessons and Timetable designed by Mary were firmly established in the school as was the Monitor system. In addition, Agnes' report of the first day of classes indicates well-disciplined pupils and a steady atmosphere. Teresa, an experienced teacher in Mary's methods, was well able to take over the management and the teaching from Annie MacKillop and Julia Fitzgerald. Agnes,

2. McDonald to MacKillop 13.5.1868.
3. Smith to McMullen, 4.5.1868.
4. Mary left Penola on 8 May. Penola Diary. McDonald to MacKillop, 13.5.1868.

untrained and inexperienced, was full of good will and enthusiasm for the task ahead.

With Mary MacKillop's departure, the two novices faced the challenge of learning how to be religious, and in particular Sisters of St Joseph. Isolated as they were from other Sisters, they were guided by the instruction given by the co-founders. Thus they gave priority to faithful following of the Rule, careful attention to the diary and frequent writing to Mary MacKillop and Father Woods. This is borne out by Teresa's words to Mary after only a few weeks at Penola. '... we are very busy but manage to keep our Rule pretty well. I think we try to say our Office at the proper time. We are very anxious to do all our holy Rule prescribes. We know on that our happiness depends.'[5]

And both Sisters were very happy at Penola. A string of letters tells of Agnes' bubbly, outgoing personality and Teresa, knowing that Agnes enjoyed writing newsy letters, left most of the detailed reporting to her.[6] By contrast, Teresa's letters, often short but still revealing her cheerful disposition, contain a reserved and serious edge. It was still very early days for the Institute. She was conscious that some of the people, including several priests, looked with suspicion upon the newly-founded Australian group which did not observe all the traditions of European Religious Orders. There was also doubt as to the Sisters' teaching ability and to the viability of the Catholic school system which Father Woods was still in the process of establishing.[7] It was essential therefore that every Josephite community conduct itself with dignity and in strict accordance with the Rule as written by Father Woods. It was the same for the schools. Only through their 'fruits' would the people and the priests come to respect the Sisters and value the schools. Aware of this and deeply committed to the success of the Institute and the schools, Teresa was determined that the Penola convent and school would be without reproach. As she wrote to Mary, '[we] try to improve every day.'[8] To Father Woods she

---

5. McDonald to MacKillop, 25.5.1868.
6. There are some fifteen extant letters written by Agnes to Mary MacKillop between 9 May and 29 November 1868.
7. Mother Mary of the Cross MacKillop, *Julian Tenison Woods: A Life*, Canonisation edition introduced and annotated by Margaret Press (Strathfield, Australia: St Pauls, 2010), 87–93.
8. McDonald to MacKillop, 27.5.1868.

spoke of her faith that all would be well with the Penola community and school: 'You must not fear for us. We are all St Joseph's.'[9]

Both the Sisters were well received in Penola. In keeping with the Rule their convent was without revenue. Accordingly they charged no schools fees, and received only the little money that some parents were able to provide. Many of the people, however, were extremely generous in other ways. '. . . half a sheep and a pound of butter,'[10] 'a brace of ducks'[11] and 'a bottle of milk'[12] were among the first gifts to the Sisters. Teresa summed up this generosity when she wrote to Father Woods that 'the people are very kind.'[13]

Life for Teresa and Agnes soon settled into a pattern. According to the Rule they rose at 5am and as there was no oratory in their few rooms at the back of the school house, they went to the church for Morning Prayer and Meditation. When the parish priest, Father O'Connor, was away on his rounds of the parish they had no Mass—sometimes for as long as three weeks.[14] The weekdays were taken up with classes. Teresa's expertise and experience came to the fore in making St Joseph's a happy and successful school. By the end of June she reported to Mary that 'the children are so good and so fond of us,' and later '[they] are improving so much.'[15] The peoples' initial scepticism of the Sisters' teaching ability disappeared as numbers on the Roll nearly doubled within six months of the first classes.[16]

While the school remained their priority, both Sisters soon realised that their work would stretch far beyond St Joseph's. Their letters provide an insight into just how involved they were in the Penola community.

One of the most time consuming aspects of that involvement was visitation of Catholics who did not attend Mass and the sacraments,

---

9. McDonald to Woods, 5.5.1868.
10. Smith to MacKillop, 9.5.1868.
11. Smith to Woods, 4.5.1868.
12. Penola Diary, 9.5.1868.
13. McDonald to Woods, 5.5.1868.
14. Smith to Woods, 19.5.1868, 29.11.1868; McDonald to Woods, 5.5.1868; McDonald to MacKillop 28.6.1868.
15. McDonald to MacKillop, 28.6.1868; October, 1868.
16. McDonald to MacKillop, October, 1868. 'We have about 70 on the roll—25 are boys.' Smith to McKillop, 16.10.1868. That number included a small percentage of non-Catholics. At some stage a third teacher, Mr Clarke, was employed at St Joseph's. Smith to MacKillop, 29.11.1868.

parents of the school children, the sick and anyone who was in need. The Diary records that on just one visit the Sisters walked 'about two miles to see a woman whose husband never goes to Communion.'[17] Even while Mary MacKillop was still with the Sisters, the mission of getting 'lapsed' Catholics to return to 'their duty' began.[18] Teresa wrote of this to Father Woods: 'If we could get three or four persons more to go to their duty I think Penola would be very well but we must pray for them very hard. How hard it is to get some people to go to their dutys' (sic).[19] Agnes also wrote of their efforts. Naming a certain man she continued: '[he] has not been to confession this long time, and it is not our fault, for we went twice and sent for him, and he said he would go but has not.'[20] Again and again both Agnes and Teresa, who evidently kept out a sharp eye for those who attended or failed to attend Mass and the sacraments, wrote of their success and sometimes failure in this regard. Indeed their earnestness in attracting people to the Catholic Church and especially in drawing back to the Church those who had fallen away from its practices attest to their kindly yet determined spirit of evangelisation.

Another pressing duty was the night school. Teresa usually taught a mixture of boys together with some aboriginal men and boys in the school room, while Agnes attended to the girls in a separate area.[21] These classes were conducted on a few nights of the week for those who for one reason or another could not attend during the day. There were also catechism classes on Sundays and when Father O'Connor was absent from the parish they led the rosary.[22] Teresa also gave special and individual instruction to those who wished to become Catholics. Among these were several aboriginal men.[23]

Then there were the many unexpected calls on their time: Teresa's making a shirt for a boy in urgent need, Teresa's dressing the blisters on a young man's neck and giving him breakfast because 'he has no one to mind him,' Teresa's making a hurried visit to a woman gravely

---

17. Penola Diary, 1.7.1868.
18. Smith to MacKillop, 4.5.1868.
19. Smith to McMullen, 4.5.1868. McDonald to Woods, 19.5.1868.
20. Smith to MacKillop, 17.6.1868.
21. Smith to MacKillop, 17.6.1868; 29.6.1868; 16.10.1868. McDonald to MacKillop, October, 1868. Penola Diary, 12.5.1868.
22. Penola Diary, 11.5.1868.
23. McDonald to MacKillop, 25.5.1868. Friday, May, 1868.

ill, Teresa's listening to a desperate woman whose house was to be 'sold out,' both Sisters abandoning meditation to attend a sick call, both Sisters minding a lady's small children so that she could attend confession and Mass.[24] There were also the regular household tasks: washing the clothes, cooking the meals, cleaning, maintaining the vegetable garden, fruit trees and flower garden. Added to these duties was the weekly cleaning of the church and the presbytery kitchen.[25] But there were also the light moments: the antics of the four kittens which had been given to the Sisters, Teresa's having to hide her face so that her pupils would not see her laughing at some of their answers in class, the visits of the MacKillop and Cameron families and the gift of a bunch of violets to Agnes from a 'dear little child.'[26]

In the midst of all this activity, both Josephite novices continued to observe all the regulations of the Rule regarding prayer, meditation and spiritual reading. Teresa had the added responsibility of training Agnes in the religious life and in the skills of teaching. It is no surprise that nearly every letter penned from the Penola convent included the words, 'we are very busy.' When one considers that Agnes had joined the Institute only a few weeks prior to arriving at Penola and that Teresa had only six months' experience, it is remarkable that they prayerfully, fruitfully and successfully lived the religious life, conducted St Joseph's School and unstintingly responded to the needs of the people.

But for Teresa this was not achieved without difficulty. Early in June—about a month after Mary MacKillop had returned to Adelaide—she became ill. The exact nature of the illness remains unknown. In Kapunda she had problems with her eyes. This certainly recurred during her last years but was not mentioned while she was at Penola. Teresa wrote to Mary that she 'became weaker every day', developed a severe cold and was 'scarcely able to hold the pen.'[27] So poorly did she look that the parish priest, Father O'Connor, ordered her to eat meat on the days of abstinence prescribed by the Rule—

---

24. Penola Diary, 15.5.1868, McDonald to MacKillop 15.5.1868; Saturday, June, 1868; McDonald to Woods, 19.5.1868.
25. Penola Diary, 25.6.1868, McDonald to Woods, 19.5.1868, McDonald to MacKillop, 25.5.1868.
26. Smith to MacKillop, 29.5.1868, Smith to Sister Ignatius O'Brien, 29.6.1868.
27. McDonald to MacKillop, Saturday, June, 1868.

Wednesdays and Saturdays—and provided her with some quinine and wine.[28] The following day Agnes recorded in the Diary that Teresa was 'very ill' and that she herself was 'afraid of taking the fever.'[29] For her part, Teresa wrote that she was 'quite ashamed of myself' and within a few weeks declared she would 'be strong soon.'[30] In fact, she never recovered completely from that illness.

Towards the end of 1868, Teresa made her first profession. This involved the taking for one year of the vows of poverty, chastity and obedience as well as a fourth vow 'to do all in [her] power to promote the love of Jesus, Mary and Joseph, in the hearts of little children.'[31] Teresa added the blue monogram to her habit feeling very proud but somewhat humbled. 'What do you think? I am wearing the monogram since yesterday. 'Poor me! I am not at all prepared to make my profession. I am so lacking in everything that's holy . . .' she wrote to Sister Gertrude, her companion of Kapunda days.[32]

While the letters written from the Penola convent and the Diary entries present an excellent account of the day-to-day life of the Sisters, what further insights might they provide regarding the woman, the Josephite Sister Teresa McDonald?

As we have seen above, Teresa gave priority to fidelity both to keeping the Rule and to the spirit of the Rule. On its first pages, Father Woods clearly set out the meaning of living the spirit of that Rule:

> They [the Sisters] must be poor, humble and consider themselves the least among all religious orders . . . their highest ambition must be to remain unknown and poor . . . [they] must never forget that they come to give themselves wholly to God. They must belong completely to Him. Their whole desire must be to love God and to love nothing else, neither friends, riches, comforts, worldly news, nor even worldly knowledge; and, finally, they

---

28. Smith to MacKillop, 17.6.1868.
29. Penola Diary, 18.5.1868.
30. McDonald to MacKillop, 28 June, 1868.
31. McDonald to Hayman, 22.11.1868. Woods, *Rules of the Institute of St Joseph*, 4. Register of the Sisters of St Joseph.
32. McDonald to Hayman, 22.11.1868. All professed Sisters of St Joseph wore on the bodice of their habits a blue monogram symbolising Mary, the mother of Jesus together with three J's, in honour of Jesus, St Joseph and St John the Baptist.

must cease to love their own wills, and learn to be subject to
all, for the love of God.[33]

These were high ideals which reflected both the understanding of
religious life during Woods' time and the Josephite spirit of poverty
and humility. The standard set before all Religious was no less than
perfection. For the Sisters of St Joseph this included perfection in
living out their particular spirit. When Teresa joined the Institute she
took with her not only her unique personality but also her experience
of social attitudes to women. That was the context from which she
moved into a way of life which named humility as its particular spirit.
All these factors came into play when, inexperienced and with little
training in the religious life, Teresa arrived in Penola in 1868. From
the beginning, her letters give a strong sense of her pursuit of this
virtue. She wrote to Father Woods:

> Do for pity's sake pray for me. I never wanted it more than
> now. I don't know what today. I wish I could say what I feel.
> I must ask our Blessed Lord to tell you Himself. I am sure he
> will but don't think me good. I wonder how it is he permits me
> to pass for what I am not. All the people think such beautiful
> things about us, it humbles me dreadfully when I know
> differently.[34]

Three days later she wrote to Mary MacKillop: 'Everything helps
to make me know my nothingness.'[35] When asking Mary to write to
Agnes, she adds: 'never mind me.'[36] She writes again to Mary: 'when
can my unworthy actions please Him? They are so mixed up with self
and altogether so badly performed.'[37] At the time of her profession
she declared: 'I am so lacking in everything that's holy.'[38] These few
words, typical of her writing, open a window into Teresa's inner story.
At the very time that her actions showed her to be a prudent and
inspiring leader totally trusting in God's love and committed to the
care of those around her, she seemed to be underrating that trust and

---

33. Woods, *Rules of the Institute of St Joseph*, 1–2.
34. McDonald to Woods, 19.5.1868.
35. McDonald to MacKillop, 21.5.1868.
36. McDonald to MacKillop, Saturday, June, 1868.
37. McDonald to MacKillop, September or October, 1868.
38. McDonald to Hayman, 22.11.1868.

devaluing her motives. It must be remembered, however, that Teresa was not alone in having such attitudes. The letters of the Sisters— especially during those early years of the Institute—reveal similar dispositions. Encouraged by their Spiritual Director, directed by their Rule and reflecting Catholic spirituality of the time, they pursued and practised the virtue of humility as understood within that context. While to modern ears Teresa's words might suggest an unhealthy self-deprecation, their true meaning can be appreciated only by placing them within a broad context. Nonetheless, it was during her time at Penola that humility emerged as foundational to Teresa's spirituality.

Other major characteristics of Teresa's spirituality had been evident when she was stationed at Kapunda. Compassion had motivated her to speak of the Sisters' illness to Father Woods. At Penola she was unstinting in her tender-heartedness, kindness and care for anyone in need as she continued to give expression to a deep compassion founded in love for God and others. That compassion, together with the virtue of humility, lay at the heart of her spirituality.

Irrespective of such rich, empowering and motivating forces, one wonders how Teresa managed to attend to the school and to all the other calls on her time when she obviously suffered from ill health. That she did so speaks of an intelligent, capable and efficient woman. And of course she had—as her Josephite Sister and assistant—the willing, generous and joyful Sister Agnes.

As the year 1868 drew to a close, the Sisters decided to hold a special celebration in honour of the feast of the Immaculate Conception.[39] A local newspaper carried a vivid description of the 'beautiful banners' and the 'statuette of the Virgin borne by four boys in white' which led the procession of nearly 100 children through the streets of Penola. A few days later, the annual school examinations were held by the parish priest, Father O'Connor, and the Board of Management. Answers to questions in history, geography, grammar and arithmetic were 'ready and correct.' The examiners were pleased also with the 'handsome' display of needle, wool and bead work. Throughout the whole procedure the 'pupils were well behaved, and

---

39. The Immaculate Conception is a Catholic teaching which holds that Mary, the mother of Jesus, was free from sin from the first moment of her existence. The feast of the Immaculate Conception is celebrated on 8 December.

their teachers had them under complete control.' The distribution of prizes was followed by a picnic.[40]

Within a few days, Teresa and Agnes prepared to go to Adelaide to celebrate Christmas, to holiday briefly together and to make a retreat. Teresa seems to have been aware that she would not be returning to Penola. Towards the end of the year she wrote: 'I shall be sorry to leave St Joseph's. It is a pretty little Church, and it was here I had so many proofs of His watchfulness over us.'[41] She had been in the Institute thirteen months, made her first Profession, successfully taken over and conducted the Penola school and established a strong and fruitful Josephite presence in the town. Above all, Teresa had known the watchful, loving presence of the God to whom she had given her all. It had been seven months since she made that long journey from Kapunda to Adelaide and thence to Penola. As she prepared to leave for Adelaide, she was unaware that this journey would be taking her into an impending crisis which would result in the near-destruction of the Institute.

Teresa of the Incarnat.

40. *Border Watch*, 21.12.1868.

41. McDonald to Hayman, 22.11.1868. There is no extant documentation which provides the details of Teresa's move to Adelaide. However, the contents of Teresa's letter written in early May 1869 to Mary MacKillop from the Franklin Street Convent indicate that she was Little Sister in Adelaide. McDonald to MacKillop, 1.5.1869. That Teresa was in Adelaide by May 1869 is confirmed by Sister Angela Carroll. Carroll to MacKillop, 12.5.1869.

7

A Move To Adelaide

About the same time as Teresa arrived in Adelaide, Bishop Sheil returned from Europe bringing with him a community of Dominican nuns. As no arrangements had been made for the new arrivals' accommodation, Mary MacKillop offered them the cottages in Franklin Street occupied by the Josephites and arranged for her own Sisters to move into a small rented house in Gouger Street. Thus it was that by Christmas 1868, Teresa had settled into Gouger Street.

Other changes had taken place during the time Teresa spent in Penola. Although Bishop Sheil had been absent from the diocese for most of 1867 and all of 1868, Father Woods had kept him well informed about the Josephites. His glowing reports of their increase in numbers and work in the schools convinced Sheil of the viability and necessity of 'this invaluable organisation.'[1] By the time he returned to Adelaide he had decided to give his approval of the Josephite Rule for use within his diocese. This was given on 17 December 1868. The Institute thus had an official standing within the diocese.

Another change that had taken place during Teresa's absence was the rapid growth of the Institute. During 1868, forty young women had joined the Josephites bringing the total number by the end of that year to fifty.[2] Although at least half of that number would have been living in convents scattered across the countryside, the Gouger Street convent was overcrowded. Early in 1869 Bishop Sheil offered them the use of a more suitable house near to where they had previously lived in Franklin Street. This meant another move for Teresa.

---

1. Sheil to Woods, 28.4.1868.
2. Foale, *The Josephite Story*, 234.

It was also early in 1869 that a decision was made by the Catholic Education Commission to build a school especially for those children whose parents were unable to pay fees. Situated in Franklin Street it was known as the Poor School. When the accommodation provided for the Sisters earlier in the year proved insufficient an upper storey, consisting of a living area and chapel, was added to the Poor School. By June of that year it was ready for occupation and Teresa and her companions were able to enjoy the extra space.[3]

Although there are no extant records which give specific reasons for Teresa's move from Penola to Adelaide, there are indications that she was appointed Little Sister in the Franklin Street community and to teach at the Poor School.[4] Mary MacKillop was spending more and more time in the country convents and schools instructing her Sisters in the Josephite Rule and the religious life, as well as training them in teaching method. She needed a reliable, wise and competent Sister in charge of the main Josephite house in Adelaide in order to lead the community of some sixteen Sisters and to assist in the initial training of the postulants and novices. Also in the community were the twenty-three-year old Sister Ignatius O'Brien, who had joined the Institute in February 1868 and Sister Angela Carroll who turned sixteen just after her entry in July 1868. Angela assisted Teresa in the Poor School while Ignatius seemed to have some level of authority in the community.[5] Both these Sisters were professed during 1869—Ignatius in March and Angela in August.[6] They were to play significant roles in the difficulties which would emerge as the months passed and into which Teresa would be drawn. But irrespective of Mary MacKillop who was Sister Guardian, or of the Little Sisters in the various convents, Father Woods maintained his authority in the Institute. He decided all matters of policy, appointed the Sisters to their convents and work and as Father Director was their spiritual guide.

---

3. Osmund Thorpe, *Mary MacKillop*, (third edition) (Sydney: Sisters of St Joseph of the Sacred Heart, 1994), 68–69.
4. McDonald to MacKillop, 1.5.1869.
5. In a letter to Mary MacKillop on 1.5.1868, Teresa refers to Ignatius going from Franklin Street to the Refuge for 'a week or so' in order to settle some matters with the Little Sister, Sister Gertrude.
6. Foale, *The Josephite Story*, 62.

Throughout 1869 Teresa's presence in the Franklin Street convent meant that she was on hand when Mary MacKillop returned in between her visits to the country Sisters. Father Woods also was in Adelaide. This accounts for the lack of correspondence between the three and hence a dearth of extant material covering the events, discussions and decisions of the year. However, certain developments within the diocese ensured that 1869 was not uneventful in Teresa's story.

As explained in Chapter Five, the Catholic schools throughout the Colony of South Australia were in a poor state at the beginning of the 1860s. The appointment of Father Woods as Director General of Catholic Education and the availability of the Sisters of St Joseph to staff both existing and new schools offered a solution to this problem. Such was the pressure from the bishop, priests and parents who desired Catholic education for Catholic children, and the desire of both Woods and Mary MacKillop to provide it, that Sisters inadequately trained in both the religious life and teaching were appointed to the task.

But as the months of 1869 passed, rumbles of discontent could be heard in the diocese. Because of the rapid increase in the number of schools and Woods and Mary MacKillop's stipulations that there be an experienced teacher in each community, Sisters were constantly on the move.[7] When they had no money for fares, they asked the local people to cover the cost. Some of the priests considered that the generosity of their parishioners to the Josephites was causing a decline in their already small parish collections. In addition, they were displeased by the disruption of classes caused by the frequent exchange of teachers, some of whom they regarded incompetent in both theological and educational matters. Some priests also had other concerns about the Sisters—their practice of begging from door to door for their own upkeep as well as for such institutions as the Refuge, and the fact that they did not conform to all the traditions of European Religious Orders.[8] Indeed, in some quarters there was a growing feeling that the Sisters, whose Rule stipulated that they

---

7. MacKillop to Woods, 2.11.1869; McDonald to MacKillop, 1.5.1869.
8. Sister Bernard Walsh to MacKillop, 24.11.1870.

own no property or take no school fees except from those who could afford them, were becoming 'a burden to the diocese.'[9]

Another cause for the growing discontent in the diocese was Father Woods. As Director of Catholic Education he was authorised by the bishop to develop a Catholic education system within the diocese and oversee the schools. In his unlimited trust in Divine Providence, invincible optimism and zeal, he forged ahead without due regard for lack of finance or for the untrained Josephites whom he appointed to staff the schools. As Margaret Press succinctly put it, 'He was intuitive rather than logical, his feelings usually dictating his line of action as well as the rationalisation of those actions later.'[10] Compounding the situation were the Sisters' lack of finance and Woods' determination that on no account should religious poverty, one of the central tenets of the Josephite Rule, be compromised. His spiritual direction of the Sisters also raised questions. Given to a mystical and imaginative spirituality, his belief that he was personally and directly inspired by God and Mary the mother of Jesus resulted in imprudence and rashness in his direction of some the Sisters. In particular it allowed him to be unduly influenced by two Sisters who claimed to have supernatural experiences.[11]

Throughout 1869 the circumstances of the Sisters and Father Woods spilled into each other creating mounting criticism and discontent among some of the clergy. The Sisters too felt uneasy. Such was the backdrop against which Teresa carried out her duties in the Franklin Street convent and the Poor School. A crisis was all that was necessary for the situation to erupt. The first signs of this began to emerge in the last months of the year.

It was in October that Bishop Sheil and Bishop James Quinn of Brisbane set out on the long journey to Rome for the Vatican Council. Before leaving Australian waters, Quinn sent a letter to Father Woods requesting a community of Josephites for Queensland. It was

9. Foale, *The Josephite Story*, 50.
10. Margaret Press, *Julian Tenison Woods: Father Founder*, (second edition) (North Blackburn: Collins Dove, 1994), 247.
11. Woods to MacKillop, 22.4.1870. The two Sisters were Ignatius O'Brien and Angela Carroll. For more information on the causes and level of discontent within the diocese see Press, *Julian Tenison Woods*, chapter 8; Foale, *The Josephite Story*, chapter 3; Osmund Thorpe, *Mary MacKillop*, chapter 7.

authorised by Sheil who added: 'See to this as soon as possible. Take Sister Mary and begin the good work.'[12]

The arrangements for the first foundation outside South Australia began immediately. In agreement with Sheil's order Mary MacKillop was to accompany the Sisters to Queensland. As well as the makeup of the foundation, Woods and Mary's deliberations also included the question of who would fill the positions of authority in Adelaide during Mary's absence. The whole matter seemed to be of concern to Mary—especially about her being absent from Adelaide for an extended period. She confided in Woods: 'I have such a strange thought about Queensland . . . it is something about my not remaining there so long.'[13] For his part Woods continued to assure her: 'It is true our care and vigilance is of use to prevent us neglecting duties and doing wrong, but prudence is of no use to me whatever. I see so plainly that we are in the arms of Mary and she carries us hither and thither just as she wills.'[14] By that time Woods was even more favourably disposed to the two Sisters—Angela and Ignatius—who claimed supernatural visitations of both divine and demonic origin. Although Mary at first showed some reverence for what she regarded as their holiness, she seems to have thought that one way of dealing with them might be to send one or both to Queensland.[15] Woods, however, would not hear of it. Such was his desire that they remain in Adelaide that he advised Mary he was 'under obedience to the Bishop' to keep both Sisters in Adelaide until his return from Rome.[16] In the New Year he appointed them to significant positions in the Institute—Ignatius as Little Sister at Franklin Street and the 17-year-old Angela as Mistress of Novices. Among the several names that the co-founders considered for the new foundation and for office in Adelaide was Teresa McDonald. In the end she was appointed to the office of Provincial in South Australia. Mary MacKillop was to remain Sister Guardian.

At the end of 1869, Bishop Sheil had already been away from the diocese since October. In charge during his absence was the Vicar

---

12. James Quinn to Sheil, 18.10.1869. Cited in Thorpe, *Mary MacKillop*, 71. Bishop Quinn had heard about the Josephites when he attended the second Provincial Synod of Bishops in Melbourne earlier in the year.
13. MacKillop to Woods, 2.11.1869.
14. Woods to MacKillop, 3.11.1869.
15. MacKillop to Woods, 9.11.1869 ; 18.11.1869; 23.11.1869.
16. Woods to MacKillop, 7.11.1869.

General, Father John Smyth. Father Woods continued to be the object of clergy grievances and to be deluded and deceived by the small group of Sisters who had come to be known as the 'visionaries.'[17] The Sisters of St Joseph numbered eighty-two, including thirty-six professed Sisters, thirty-five novices and eleven postulants.[18] Their Superior or Provincial was the 31-year-old Teresa McDonald who had joined the Institute just two years and two months prior to that appointment. The foundation bound for Brisbane left Adelaide on 8 December 1869. With Mary's departure, the Adelaide community was deprived of the practical common sense and prudent leadership of the co-foundress at a time when it was desperately needed. Years later Mary MacKillop reflected on that time and set of circumstances: 'And so the storm gathered.'[19]

Teresa of the Incarnat[...]

17. Others in the visionary group were: Sisters Helena Myles, Sebastian Fitzgerald, Paula Green and Julian Brown.
18. Foale, *The Josephite Story*, 56.
19. MacKillop, *Julian Tenison Woods*, 130.

8
Provincial In South Australia

Teresa's first task as Provincial was to welcome all the Sisters to Franklin Street for the annual retreat. Though 'quite edified by the behaviour and attention paid by our Sisters,' her 'poor cold heart' seemed unmoved throughout the days. She was, in fact, having difficulty settling into her new position. ' . . . I have not seen nor do I yet understand my duties,' she wrote to Mary in Brisbane. 'I am not myself at all these times. I feel quite a stranger,' she added.[1]

The Brisbane Sisters had gone for only a month when Teresa began to look forward to Mary's return. 'Thanks be to our God you will soon come home again,' she wrote to the Sister Guardian whom she missed as both friend and guide.[2] But the many tasks of her new office lay before her and there was no time to waste. There were the arrangements for the Sisters to return to their convents, matters to do with school supplies and a disagreement regarding the school marking system to be resolved. A number of bills needed attention and there were those in need—women and children—whom Teresa tried to assist with food and clothing. Saturdays were spent writing to the country Sisters—a task she considered important if she was to foster that sense of unity essential to Josephite life.[3] Once school commenced she was occupied with classes at the North Adelaide school. With seventy children on the roll, Teresa and the other member of staff, Sister Ursula, were fully occupied. The Refuge, the

---

1. McDonald to MacKillop, 3.1.1870.
2. McDonald to MacKillop, 3.1.1870.
3. McDonald to MacKillop, 13.2.1870.

Orphanage and the Bay Providence, for which she had a special care, were all going well.[4]

Although Teresa would have been well aware of Sisters Ignatius and Angela's supposed mystical experiences during the previous year, she seems to have begun 1870 with a desire to make a new beginning with her two Sisters. Early in the year she reported to Brisbane: 'S. Ignatius getting very good health, and also S. Angela and so good. She asked me to be her Mother the other day and we are great friends.'[5] But already the Provincial was concerned about Franklin Street. As the Mother House in which the postulants and novices, a large community of professed Sisters as well as occasional visiting Sisters were housed, it required a kind, patient and caring Little Sister. Teresa knew that on some occasions, Ignatius failed to bring those qualities to the position.[6]

Towards the end of January there was an incident during the night in the Franklin Street chapel. Teresa found Sisters Ignatius and Angela reduced to an insensible state with flames playing around their eyes. Practical by nature, she did not know what to make of such an unusual display. She was both curious and yet 'did not like to pry into the designs of God.' She asked Angela to pray to the Blessed Mother that she might understand what had happened. The following evening Father Woods arrived with a message for Teresa from 'our beautiful Mother' written in Angela's hand. Full of numerous expressions of loving care, it assured the Provincial that even if she 'sometimes fails in not performing the duties which her office extracts of her,' God would be glorified in the end. Teresa was not convinced. 'I had my doubts . . . I felt strange . . . I don't feel comfortable,' she wrote. A few nights later there was another incident when the blanket on Teresa's bed was burnt. This filled her with fear. 'I am afraid every time I awake,' she wrote to Mary MacKillop, adding, 'do oh pray hard for me.'[7] Meanwhile, the supposedly heavenly and/or demonic visitations in the convent and surrounds continued and Father Woods' delight in such marvels grew.[8]

---

4. McDonald to MacKillop, 29.1.1870.
5. McDonald to MacKillop, 3.1.1870.
6. McDonald to MacKillop, 13.2.1870; 20.2.1870.
7. McDonald to Mackillop, 29.1.1870.
8. Woods to MacKillop, 11.4.1870.

While her suspicions about Ignatius and Angela increased and she berated herself for a lack of charity, Teresa forged ahead with her work.[9] Her experience at the North Adelaide school persuaded her that the area would benefit greatly from the presence of the Sisters. She set her mind to establishing a convent near the school. The severe economic downturn in Adelaide in 1870 also presented a challenge to a Provincial whose care extended to all the Josephite convents, schools and charitable institutions. Such was the poverty that the Sisters 'could not beg enough bread for the Refuge.'[10] Her other challenge was to provide accommodation for the young women seeking entrance to the Institute. 'I don't know what we shall do with all the candidates,' she wrote to the Sister Guardian. There is no doubt that Teresa found both her duties and her fear and concern regarding the strange happenings at Franklin Street a heavy burden. She wrote to Mary far away in Queensland: 'I am thinking you will soon be back again among us and then, oh may I resign my present office . . . I am almost done up, indeed I wonder I am able to keep up.'[11]

Mary MacKillop, however, could do little about the Mother House situation except advise Teresa to speak to Woods and write concerned letters to him advising prudence.[12] His replies did nothing to reassure her. The devil was behind all the strange happenings and God was allowing this 'cross' for his sanctification and that of the Sisters. There was no cause for 'uneasiness' because the Blessed Mother could not fail her children.[13] Yet irrespective of her misgivings the Sister Guardian reminded the Sisters that she was 'bound to obey' the Father Director and so were they.[14]

It was not until the Tuesday of Easter week that the situation reached crisis point. On that day the tabernacle in the chapel was rifled and spots of blood could be seen on the altar cloth. As Woods, Smyth and 'all the other clergymen . . . examined the place,' the distraught and mystified Sisters waited. Teresa became so ill she had to leave the chapel. The following day there were fires in the convent and the

9. McDonald to MacKillop, 13.2.1870.
10. McDonald to MacKillop, 20.2.1870.
11. McDonald to MacKillop, 13.2.1870.
12. MacKillop to Woods, 5.3.1870; 16.3.1870; 6.4.1870.
13. Woods to MacKillop, 22.4.1870.
14. MacKillop to O'Brien, 7.4.1870.

classroom. So upset was Teresa that only on her third attempt did she manage to write a coherent report to Mary. 'We have just passed through a whole sea of Sorrows,' she wrote. Three days later Woods told the Sisters that 'no human hand had removed the BS but God for His own wise designs . . . .' On the other hand the Vicar General, Father Smyth, announced that an ecclesiastical investigation would be held into the happening. This unnerved Teresa who, as she 'anxiously awaited our trial,' became more apprehensive. Little wonder that the fearful, bewildered Provincial concluded her letter to Mary with the request: 'Would you hurry home . . . .'.[15] For several weeks, however, the Father Director had been advising Mary: 'I cannot say anything about your coming to South Australia for a while. I believe it is not the Will of God at present.'[16]

It was after Easter that the situation with Ignatius deteriorated. The Sisters began to complain to Teresa that the Little Sister was always finding fault with them and reminding them of their duty in little things, while in several areas she did not keep the Rule herself.[17] After Woods advised Teresa to speak to Ignatius, she tried to raise the matter in a 'gentle manner.' This resulted in 'many misunderstandings' between the two Sisters and tension which never seemed to be resolved. It was a difficult situation for Teresa because she knew Woods believed that the two visionaries were highly favoured by God and that the devil was the instigator of the strange incidents in the convent. As community life became more disrupted and the Sisters more unhappy, Teresa became more troubled. Reflecting on the situation she suggested to Mary MacKillop that 'perhaps it is my own fault. I am so much from home, and when I come I am so tired.'[18]

During this time when Teresa seems to have been still teaching at North Adelaide, she had another responsibility that through the months was to prove very demanding. Sister Rose Cunningham, who had been Mary MacKillop's first companion at Penola, became so disturbed by 1870 that she had to be kept under almost constant

15. McDonald to MacKillop, 21.4.1870. The full report of this incident was contained in this letter.
16. Woods to MacKillop, 11.4.1870.
17. McDonald to MacKillop, 12.6.1870; McMullen to MacKillop, 25.6.1870; MacKillop to Woods 8.7.70.
18. McDonald to MacKillop, 12.6.1870.

surveillance. This task fell largely to Teresa who, when she was not occupied in school, somehow managed to cope with Rose. During her Sister's better times, Teresa took her for short holidays to the country convents. Noting Teresa's devoted care of Rose, Josephine McMullen commented: 'Poor T stays with her all the time when she is at home.'[19] 'Poor Sr Teresa has a heavy cross in her.'[20] The Provincial, whose health had never completely recovered since the illness in Penola, carried a heavy load of work, the worry of Franklin Street and the wearing presence of Rose.

That was not all. Teresa wrote of her 'awful repugnant feelings and dislikes' towards the Father Director and of her inability to speak much to him.[21] Speculation suggests that his belief and trust in the visionaries, and the deference and compassion he showed them fuelled these feelings. Teresa seems to have had a depth of discernment and quality of common sense whereby she saw through the deceit of her Sisters. That the Father Director did not, led to frustration and 'awful repugnant feelings and dislikes' towards him. This caused her to feel intense guilt or as she put it, 'dreadful pain of mind.'[22] After all, he was their highly respected Father Director—a priest held in deep affection by the Sisters. In addition, she sympathised with him in the difficulties she knew he was experiencing—'Poor FD has many crosses and not many to share with him'—and this intensified the guilt she felt in her feelings of dislike towards him.[23] That guilt added to her burdens.

As this mix of emotions, the demands of teaching and of Rose increased, Teresa felt more inadequate and unable to manage. Early in July she told Mary:

> I am and have been in such dreadful pain of mind, what with my duties and disturbed mind and awful repugnant feelings and dislikes to FD and the Sisters. I have passed through a little purgatory and I cannot help them. I am quite willing to suffer any pain as long as I do not offend our sweet Lord

19. McMullen to MacKillop, 25.6.70.
20. McMullen to MacKillop, 8.8.1870. Rose was not admitted into the Adelaide Lunatic Asylum until 19 July, 1871. Foale, *The Josephite Story*, 31–32.
21. McDonald to MacKillop, 12.6.1870; 3.7.1870.
22. McDonald to MacKillop, 3.7.1870.
23. McDonald to MacKillop, 3.7.1870.

and Master and I trust I shall with the aid of His grace battle on. I told you in one of my letters some of my troubles . . . I shall state . . . all my anxieties and fears about my Sisters and the rule and myself. You know I was from the scrub and placed in S. Mary's place in Adelaide convent, and as I did not understand the dispositions of my Sisters, I began to fear, and I suppose M. Horney helped me to be troubled. I could not tell much to FD as he seemed to think I was complaining. S. Angela and Ignatius were in temptation, one against the other, so that I felt all was wrong. I suppose too that I did not do my duty as I did not point out to them in what they broke the rule. I am to blame I know that now.[24]

In view of Teresa's words the question arises of just how suited she was to the position of Provincial. For a start her health was against such a demanding position and it has been suggested that she 'lacked confidence in her ability as leader.'[25] But the question remains: Did she lack confidence in her leadership ability or did circumstances in Adelaide and the actions of Father Woods gradually disallow what leadership qualities she may have had? After all, though she was not the Little Sister in Kapunda, she assumed a responsible role in writing to Woods regarding the Sisters' damaging fast. In Penola she managed well in charge of the school and as Little Sister. When she first assumed the position of Provincial she made it clear that she did not understand what was entailed in the appointment.[26] One wonders if she was aware of the directives in the Rule regarding the role and authority of the Provincial. It stated:

> Each Province shall be governed by a Sister Provincial, who shall, under the Bishop, or his representative, regulate the affairs of the communities of the Province. Out of Chapter time she may give her permission to the removal of Sisters from house to house, receive postulants, establish new

---

24. McDonald to MacKillop, 3.7.1870. FD referred to the Father Director, (Father Woods), the 'scrub' refers to Penola, 'Horney' is the name for the devil frequently used by Woods and the Sisters.
25. Foale, *The Josephite Story*, 61.
26. McDonald to MacKillop, 3.1.70.

foundations, and watch over the general observance of the rule throughout the Province.[27]

The Rule, however, was very new and those committed to it young in the religious life. In addition, Teresa's appointment as Provincial was the first of its kind in an Institute which was still finding its way. It could have been that in such an inexperienced group the practical application of some details of the Rule were not fully understood. Father Woods' authority in the Institute seems to have developed gradually, and to some extent, naturally: his priestly office gave him a superior position, he was co-founder of the Institute and its spiritual director, and he had sole authority over the schools. From the beginning Mary MacKillop had deferred to his authority although she certainly presented her opinions and as difficulties arose tried to advise him. But as he became more convinced of his God-given authority over the Institute, he gradually assumed control. By April 1870 he wrote to Mary: 'I declare most solemnly in the presence of God ... I believe I am the chosen instrument to guide the Sisters, and God will give me all necessary light and grace.'[28] With Mary in far off Queensland, that control became total. Again and again his letters to Mary listed the actions he had taken—seemingly without any reference to Teresa.[29] According to the Rule, Teresa's task as Provincial was to exercise her authority over 'the affairs of the communities of the Province', 'to watch over the general observance of the rule throughout the Province' and to be accountable to 'the Bishop or his representative.' Woods' task—given that he seemed to be the bishop's representative—was to assist her in the exercise of that authority. Instead of this, he ignored her office in the Institute and, when she tried to speak to him, gave her the impression that he thought she was complaining.

As Woods' authority became more complete and the situation at the Mother House more disturbing, Teresa's distress increased. Thus she wrote to Mary of her 'disturbed mind', of 'dreadful pain of mind', of the 'little purgatory' she experienced, of

---

27. Woods, *Rules of the Institute of St Joseph*, 12.
28. Woods to MacKillop, 22.4.1870.
29. Woods to MacKillop 11.4.1870; 22.4.1870; 4.11.1870; 12.11.1870 are just some examples.

the burden of the feelings she had for the Father Director, of her fears after her blanket was burned and of her 'duties' which included that of Provincial, the school and the care of Rose. Reflecting on the whole situation she added: 'perhaps it is my own fault,' 'I did not do my duty,' 'I know I am to blame for that.' And in explanation, or probably in deep frustration and anguish, come the words: 'I am so much from home, and when I come I am so tired.' 'I shall . . . battle on.' The gentle, kind Scotswoman struggled to withstand the confidence of the visionaries and Father Woods. If Teresa had possessed stronger leadership qualities and better health, she may well have found a way through the difficulties she faced. Foale's perceptive comment, however, draws an only possible conclusion: '. . . matters might not have reached a low point so soon if Woods had allowed her to be superior in fact as well as in name.'[30]

Though Father Woods and the Josephites continued to experience opposition in the diocese, it was not until after the Easter happenings that hostility began to increase. There were several reasons for this. Earlier in the year the Sisters at Kapunda had reported the priests of the parish—the Franciscans Horan and Keating—for serious misconduct. Father Woods took the matter to Father Smyth who dismissed Keating from the diocese. By way of revenge, Horan vowed to destroy those who had reported his friend's actions, namely Woods and the Sisters of St Joseph.[31] The Easter incident in the Franklin Street convent played into Horan's hands. But it was not only that episode and the reputation of the 'visionaries' which fuelled the fires of criticism among priests and people. Just at that troubled time, Woods announced the building of substantial extensions to the convent although he had 'no money . . . no permission to go into debt, or indeed any place to borrow it from.'[32] Though the extensions were sorely needed, this news was not well received by people battling the tough economic conditions of the time.

So the antagonism and criticism increased and the allegedly preternatural and supernatural happenings continued. Then, on the last day of June, Father Smyth died. Through the years he and Woods had shared a strong friendship and, according to Thorpe, as Vicar

---

30. Foale, *The Josephite Story*, 61.
31. Woods to MacKillop, 11.4.1670. Foale, *The Josephite Story,* 59–61.
32. Woods to MacKillop, 11.4.1870.

General he had tried to steer a middle course in the diocese during the absence of Bishop Sheil.[33] It was a crushing blow for Woods who felt that without the support of Smyth he stood alone. The Sisters too felt the loss of 'such a dear friend.'[34] Thus the diocese was left leaderless and the South Australian Josephites were still without their Sister Guardian. From Queensland came the one voice that could bring some peace and stability to the Josephites: 'I long so much to be home where I know there is much more trouble than any of you tell me.'[35]

Teresa of the Incarnate

33. Woods to MacKillop, 5.7.1870. 12.7.1870. Thorpe, *Mary MacKillop*, 82.
34. McDonald to MacKillop, 3.7.1870.
35. MacKillop to Woods, 26.5.1870.

9

From The Mother House To Mitcham

Towards the end of June 1870, some 70 Sisters gathered at the Mother House for a retreat directed by Father Woods. Teresa, who felt it had a special solemnity, was sorry when it concluded. The next day she did not go to school but stayed at the Mother House to farewell the Sisters to their various convents. Among the few changes made at the conclusion of the retreat, Teresa's old friend, Josephine McMullen, was appointed Mistress of postulants at the Mother House. Also either at some time prior to the retreat or at its conclusion, Woods appointed the 17-year-old visionary, Angela Carroll, Mistress of novices. In spite of her grave misgivings about Angela, Teresa tried to make the best of the Father Director's decision. 'S. Angela is now so attentive to her novices and attends all community exercises.' She also appeared to make a new start with Ignatius. 'All other things will, I am sure, come right soon,' she wrote to Mary.[1] The magnanimity and trust in God shown by these words, given Teresa's distressed state, while it could well indicate the measure of her powerlessness, certainly speaks highly of her charity.

It was during the retreat that the death of Father Smyth, mentioned in the previous chapter, occurred. The vacant position of Vicar General created by his death was filled by Archdeacon Patrick Russell. He immediately arranged for the long overdue investigation into the Easter happening at the Franklin Street convent. It was to be another six weeks, however, before it would take place.

In the meantime a major development occurred. Father Woods moved the Provincial (Teresa) from the Mother House to the Refuge—one of the Josephite charitable institutions situated in the

---

1. McDonald to MacKillop, 3.7.1870; McMullen to MacKillop 25.6.1870.

outer suburb of Mitcham, appointing her as Little Sister.[2] Speculation suggests three possible reasons for this move. Could it have been that Woods, aware of Teresa's worry and distress, wished to provide her with a time of rest? Given that Rose Cunningham accompanied Teresa to Mitcham, could it have been that the only way to cope with Rose was to free Teresa from her school responsibilities and appoint her to a place away from the Mother House where she could look after Rose on a full time basis? Or might it have been that Woods, influenced by Ignatius and Angela, wanted to get Teresa out of the Franklin Street convent so that his two favourites could hold complete sway in the Mother House? The context surrounding Woods' action overwhelmingly suggests that Teresa's move to the Refuge resulted from the third supposition.

Teresa settled into looking after Rose very quickly. So violent did she become that Teresa had sometimes to lock her in a room, tie her hands and get the Sisters to hold her down. Rose on other occasions escaped the Refuge reaching well into Adelaide before the Sisters found her. Even more difficult for Teresa was that Rose took a dislike to her.[3] But she did not complain, assuring Josephine that she was 'very happy.'[4] Such was the situation with Rose that Teresa was unable to attend the investigation into the Easter happenings which was held at the Mother House on 11 August. That the Provincial could be placed in such circumstances—especially as she witnessed the events—impels one to conclude that she was deliberately prevented by those who did not wish her to attend. Her inability to attend the investigation caused her some disquiet as was obvious in her report to Mary MacKillop: 'I am afraid I shall be obliged to remain at home with S. Rose, but God's holy will be done.'[5] Apart from looking after Rose, Teresa's leadership made a difference at the Refuge. The Sisters wrote to Brisbane of her calm wisdom. 'I am delighted with it (the Refuge) and wish you could see it. Sister Teresa is well fitted to be Little Sister there. She has a great fund of common sense, and though so quiet, much penetration.'[6] 'You would be delighted with the way

---

2. McDonald to MacKillop, 24.7.1870.
3. McDonald to MacKillop, 24.7.1870.
4. McDonald to McMullen, 14.7.1870.
5. McDonald to MacKillop, 14.7.1870.
6. Sister Francis Xavier Amsinck to MacKillop, 15.8.1870.

she has the Refuge.'[7] And one of the Sisters stationed at Mitcham reported on the twenty-one 'penitents' who 'are so good since Sr Teresa came out,' adding, 'we are all so happy . . . I hope she will stay for some time.'[8]

Ten priests gathered at Franklin Street for the investigation including some who were strongly opposed to Woods and the Sisters.[9] All accounts of what was obviously an ordeal for the Sisters convey the tough approach of the investigators. Woods, writing to Mary MacKillop, stressed the strength and beauty of Ignatius' answers and cruel manner in which Angela was questioned. Both Sisters, he claimed, acquitted themselves well, although Angela through constant tears.[10] Other Sisters, present at the Mother House when the event occurred, were also questioned—including Josephine McMullen. The priests' official report (which Woods did not sign) stated that 'circumstantial evidence' led them to conclude that Sister Angela had 'abstracted the Blessed Sacrament.' That report was sent to Rome.[11] Further fuelled by the Easter happenings and the manner and outcome of the investigation, criticism of the Institute grew among some of the priests and people.

Although after the retreat Teresa had high hopes of an improvement in the situation at the Mother House, it did not eventuate. Woods had not accepted the outcome of the investigation, continuing to claim that the rifling of the tabernacle 'was all the devil's work.'[12] Consequently Ignatius and Angela, together with other members of their group of visionaries, continued their deception, even after the investigation. Thus the community became more disrupted and the Rule was often ignored by some of the Sisters. Many wrote to Mary MacKillop of their fear of Ignatius, of the disregard for the Rule, some wanted Teresa back at the Mother House and most longed for the return of their Sister Guardian.[13] Even Sister Rose in one of her better

---

7. McMullen to MacKillop, September, 1870.
8. Sister Maria Healy to MacKillop, 28.8.1870.
9. McMullen to MacKillop, 14.8.1870.
10. Woods to MacKillop, 12.8.1870 cited in George O'Neil, *Life of the Reverend Julian Edmund Tenison Woods 1832–1889* (Sydney: Pellegrini & Co, 1929), 197. O'Brien to MacKillop, 16.8.1870.
11. Foale, *The Josephite Story*, 69.
12. Woods to MacKillop, 12.8.1870.
13. Walsh to MacKillop, 14.8.1870, 24.11.1870; McMullen to MacKillop, 16.8.1870,

moments begged Mary: 'Get Sister Teresa home [the Mother House] and act as Little Sister and Sister Ignatius to some other Convent.'[14] Teresa was grieved by much the Sisters told her and much that she observed when visiting the Mother House. Disregard for the Rule, the often harsh manner in which Ignatius treated the Sisters, the lack of respect among the Sisters for the Little Sister and the fear of her in the community all weighed upon the Provincial's mind. She brought up the matter with Woods who again assured her it was the devil's work. She spoke to Ignatius 'several times' about her disregard for the Rule and lack of compassion for the Sisters, but with no positive outcome. 'I am very much troubled sometimes,' she wrote to Mary. She fell ill again and was confined to bed for eleven days.[15] But always trusting in God's loving care and possibly not wanting to worry the far distant Sister Guardian, she added: 'but God is good. I think all will get better.'[16]

In Brisbane, Mary continued to worry about the situation at the Mother House. She did not approve of Ignatius and Angela's behaviour. She was also concerned that both Sisters were ignoring the Provincial, Sister Teresa. Teresa agreed with Mary. She felt that she was their immediate superior 'only in name.'[17]

These conclusions compelled Mary to speak out regarding Teresa and her position as Provincial. In a letter written early in August, she reminded Father Woods of the importance of the office of Provincial within the Institute. 'If the Sister Guardian or Provincial may not be free to act in such cases as seems best to her, believe me, dear Father, many serious evils to the Sisters and the schools will follow.'[18] Though written within the context of Queensland, these words were meant to apply also to the situation of Sister Teresa in South Australia. Apparently Mary had assumed or been given to understand that

September, 1870; 18.10.1870 and 20.11.1870; Ursula Ross to MacKillop, 16.8.1870; Healy to MacKillop, 16.8.1870, 28.8.1870; Aloysius O'Leary to MacKillop, 28.8.1870.

14. Cunningham to MacKillop, 2.8.1870.
15. Carroll to MacKillop, 18.8.1870.
16. McDonald to MacKillop, 28.8.1870.
17. MacKillop to Woods, 3.12.1871. Although Mary wrote this sometime after the period to which she was referring, it is a reflection on how she and Teresa felt during that time.
18. MacKillop to Woods, 2.8.1870.

Teresa's impending move to the Refuge was for only a short rest. In the same letter she wrote:

> Though I am glad that Sr Teresa should have a little rest, I hope that she will not have to be long away from the Mother House. I think the Sisters should lean very much upon her and that the Sisters should thoroughly understand the relative positions of herself and Sister Ignatius.

A few days later Mary was telling Woods that the Adelaide letters which had arrived that day were 'full of trouble.' Again she spoke to him of Teresa: '. . . if you can, keep Teresa in town [Mother House]. Perhaps it is not God's Will that she should be away.' This was followed by the plea: 'My Father, I would so love to see with my own eyes my Sisters and their wants.' Knowing that the Father Director believed it was not God's will that she return to Adelaide at that time and accepting he was divinely guided in this, she added: 'but blessed be the sweet Will of God which ordains otherwise.'[19] Mary even ventured to question the influence Ignatius was having over the Director stating that she 'had not sufficient confidence to believe that she [Ignatius] would always be guided by the Sacred Heart to advise only what was best for the Institute.'[20] But the Father Director took no heed of these words, viewing Mary's opinions and wishes as temptations which he encouraged her to overcome.[21]

So the letters travelled from Adelaide to Brisbane and from the Sister Guardian to the Father Director. Late in August Woods wrote a long letter answering Mary's words of concern. After discussing a number of issues to do with the schools, the object of the Institute, the criticism of the priests and his poor health he addressed her concerns regarding the Mother House. 'I am not uneasy about the Convent,' he wrote. While there were 'little irritations and suspicions' and 'faults committed,' the Sisters readily admitted these. He could not see any 'permanent character' or 'any real loss of charity' among the Mother House community.[22] Thus the situation continued—the Provincial

---

19. MacKillop to Woods, 16.8.1870.
20. MacKillop to Woods, 11.11.1870.
21. MacKillop to Woods, 11.11.1870.
22. Woods to MacKillop, 23.8.1870.

troubled and worried at Mitcham and the anxious Sister Guardian in Brisbane.

Towards the end of the year Teresa had to deal with another difficult situation regarding one of the Sisters. Sister Patrick Brazil, in her determination to leave the Institute, walked out of the Franklin Street convent. Without telling anyone of her decision, she eventually made her way to Mitcham where she hoped to meet Father Woods. Teresa, anxious as to how she could best deal with the situation, took the exhausted Sister into the convent and notified Woods. He refused to see Patrick and said she was excommunicated. But Teresa would not accept such a sentence and after a time Woods told her to try to keep the Sister at Mitcham until such time as her temporary vows had expired when she would be free to leave without requiring a dispensation. Though Patrick was still agitated and Teresa 'very anxious,' she responded to the Provincial's understanding and kindness and settled down in the Mitcham convent.[23] Teresa was full of praise for the Mitcham Sisters' patience and kindness to both Patrick and Rose—an attitude exemplified in the gentle approach shown by their Provincial. Reflecting on the demands that the condition of the two Sisters placed on Teresa and her competent yet kindly manner of caring for them, Mary MacKillop commented to Woods: 'I am sure that Sister Teresa's soul must be far advanced in the way of perfection.'[24]

Little wonder that Teresa's poor health returned towards the end of the year. From October onward she suffered from severe headaches and during that month palpitations of the heart.[25] Then in December Ignatius wrote to Mary MacKillop:

> Poor Sister Teresa is very delicate. I wish you were home as I am afraid she does not mind herself as she should do. She has been in bed for a week and when up she is as helpless as a child. She looks so wretched and careworn that it would pierce you through to look at her, but what surprises me she never complains amidst the most bitter sufferings.[26]

---

23. McDonald to MacKillop, 28.11.1870. Patrick left the Institute in 1872.
24. MacKillop to Woods, 12.12.1870.
25. McMullen to MacKillop, September, 1870; O'Brien to MacKillop, 18.10.1870.
26. O'Brien to MacKillop, 6.12.1870.

As Christmas 1870 approached, Teresa gradually improved. Work on the extensions to the convent prevented the Sisters from gathering at Franklin Street for retreat.[27] But in Adelaide and in the country convents excitement was growing at the prospect of Mary MacKillop's return from Queensland. Father Woods, who felt 'almost ready to sink' under the weight of criticism and disregard for his authority over the schools, and whose health had markedly deteriorated, also looked forward to her return.[28] In the meantime he was busy selecting another group of Sisters to send to Brisbane and finalising their passages on the steamer.

It would be March 1871 before Mary at last set out on her way to Adelaide. Meanwhile, Teresa continued at Mitcham. It had been a difficult year for the Provincial, not least for the deterioration of her health. Mary's approaching return filled her with joy. 'I have many things to say but when you come home will be better. May God speed you home to us . . .'[29]

Teresa of the Incarnate

---

27. Sister Anne McMullen to MacKillop, 14.12.1870. Woods to MacKillop, 27.12.1870. O'Brien to MacKillop, 5.10.1870. Foale, *The Josephite Story*, 77.
28. Woods to MacKillop, 27.12.1870.
29. McDonald to MacKillop, 28.11.1870.

10
A Time Of Trial

The New Year brought the news that Bishop Sheil had stopped in America on his voyage home and was expected in Adelaide on 2 February.[1] Prior to his arrival, those priests who had grievances against Father Woods and the Sisters of St Joseph had prepared a statement or memorial documenting their complaints. Underpinning the issues named was the desire to place complete control of the Sisters in each parish in the hands of the parish priest and to remove Woods from his positions of Director General of Catholic Education and Father Director of the Josephite Institute.[2] While at first Sheil dismissed the allegations of the anti-Josephite Memorial, he gradually succumbed to the priests' scheming. He dismissed the Vicar General, Archdeacon Russell. Soon Father Horan, who only the year before had determined to ruin Woods through destroying the Sisters of St Joseph, had filled the position although he was never officially appointed. Sheil then appointed Woods parish priest of North Adelaide. With Woods gone from the bishop's house and the appointment to the Adelaide parish of clergy opposed to him and the Sisters, Sheil was surrounded by those who had supported the Memorial. It was not long before his health began to fail and his mind gradually became confused. Those closest to him—Horan and his colleagues—were well placed to influence Sheil's thinking and actions.

Such was the situation when Mary finally arrived in Adelaide in April. She did, as Woods had warned her, come into 'a nest of

---

1. Woods to MacKillop, 27.12.1870; 31.1.1871.
2. Woods to MacKillop, 7.2.1871. For background information on the anti-Josephite Memorial see Foale, *The Josephite Story*, Chapters 4–5.

crosses.'[3] It was June before she was settled into the Mother House and had made a number of new appointments. Sisters Ignatius and Angela were both removed from their positions—to Mitcham and North Adelaide respectively. However Woods, still convinced of the integrity and sanctity of the visionaries, appointed both Sisters consultors to the Sister Guardian. Sister Bernard Walsh was named Provincial of South Australia and Sister Monica Phillips Mistress of Novices. Sister Teresa was to move from the Refuge at Mitcham to the Mother House where she would take up the position of Little Sister.[4]

Delighted that Mary was back in South Australia and relieved to relinquish the office of Provincial, Teresa happily settled into the Franklin Street convent.[5] Though unaware of it at the time, her position as Superior of the Mother House would draw her into a series of dramatic events which would endure into the following year and take the Institute to near destruction.

While the threats of the anti-Josephite Memorandum still hovered in the background, it was not until August that Bishop Sheil began to take a definite stand against the Sisters of St Joseph. Prior to that, Mary had set out on visitation of the country convents and schools and Woods had taken some time of rest at the Jesuit College at Sevenhill. As well as recovering from an accident and a bout of severe illness, he was aware that his debtors were closing in.[6] Matthew Quinn, Bishop of the Bathurst diocese in New South Wales, had visited asking for Sisters for the Darling River towns of Wentworth and Bourke. With Bishop Sheil's consent, it was agreed that Woods would go to Bathurst to finalise arrangements for the two foundations.[7] He left Adelaide on 1 August. Although he had expected to return within some months, it was not to be. At the end of September he wrote to Mary that Archbishop Polding had obtained permission from Sheil to keep him

3. Woods to MacKillop, 27.12.1870.
4. Woods to the Sisters, 9.6.1871; MacKillop to Woods, 8.6.1871; Woods to Sister Casimir Meskil, 9.6.1871.
5. Rose Cunningham was committed to the Adelaide Lunatic Asylum on 19 July 1871. It seems likely that Teresa would have had to stay at Mitcham until that move had taken place.
6. Woods owed some £4000 on the Refuge, the schools and for the extensions on the Franklin Street convent. Foale, *The Josephite Story*, 85.
7. MacKillop, *Julian Tenison Woods*, 152.

in New South Wales 'for some work he has for me to do.'[8] But the Father Director's years in South Australia were at an end. Except for two brief visits, he would never return.

It was late in August, after Sheil had received a letter from Rome when his attitude towards the Sisters changed. Apparently the letter was in reply to the report that had been sent to Rome regarding the Josephite visionaries and in particular the Easter happenings.[9] After admonishing the bishop for the dismissal of Russell it directed him to put his diocese in order. Although he was aware of allegations against the Josephites, Sheil was shocked by the directive from Rome. Horan and his group saw the letter as an opportunity and set about using it to their advantage. With their main objective to convince the bishop that the upkeep of the Sisters was more than the diocese could afford, that many of the Sisters were illiterate and that the priests did not have appropriate control over the Sisters, they made outrageous allegations to Sheil against the Sisters and lied about Woods. They put it to the bishop that unless he reformed the Institute, the Catholic education system within his diocese might well collapse.

It was then that Sheil acted. At first Sister Teresa had to cope with the situation alone because Mary MacKillop had been detained at the Kadina convent. Sheil had visited the Mother House with directions regarding the singing and prayers in the schools and ordering that all applicants to the Institute and postulants were to be examined by him. Teresa was particularly upset by his dismissal of a prospective postulant. 'Poor thing, she cried so much,' Teresa wrote to Mary, 'she was never at school, but could read and write a little.'[10] Teresa knew that the implementation of these directives would involve changes to the Josephite Rule. But the experienced and wise Little Sister was cautious in her dealings with Sheil because as she explained to Mary: 'I did not want to disobey his Lordship, but thought that if he gave a command it would be in a different way from the way he then acted.'[11] She was well aware that others were taking advantage of his increasingly confused state of mind.

---

8. Woods to MacKillop, 29.9.1871.
9. Foale, *The Josephite Story*, 88. For further information see Foale, *The Josephite Story*, Chapter 5.
10. McDonald to MacKillop, 3.8.1871.
11. McDonald to MacKillop, 3.8.1871.

Though worried about the turn of events with the Bishop, Teresa was not discouraged or afraid. 'I have great courage. I know we will be alright,' she wrote to Mary at Kadina.[12] The woman who as Provincial had been constrained by the Father Director and whose authority had been disregarded in favour of the visionaries had come into her own. Her responsibilities as Provincial had ceased, as had the need to care for Sister Rose. With the Sister Guardian close at hand and Woods occupied in New South Wales, Teresa had grown in confidence both in herself and as a Sister of St Joseph. She was well able to support Mary and champion the cause of the Institute in whatever troubles lay ahead.

Upon Mary's return from Kadina, Teresa accompanied her to see Bishop Sheil who had left a message that he wished to see the Sister Guardian. During the interview he listed a number of complaints against the Sisters and set out some requirements all of which involved changes in the Rule.[13] Having told Mary that all the Sisters were to move out of the Franklin Street convent and the Hall school in order that the Dominican Sisters could move in, he also ordered her to return to Kadina.[14] She was to return immediately bringing with her a Sister whom he considered 'unfit for the Institute.'

While Mary was away, Sheil informed Teresa that all the Sisters stationed in Adelaide were to assemble at the Mother House where Fathers Horan and Murphy would examine them as to their capabilities for teaching and to take an inventory of what they, the Sisters, had brought into the convent with them. The priests chose to examine only those Sisters who were employed in menial work, those

---

12. McDonald to MacKillop, 3.8.1871.

13. The following accounts, including that of the excommunication of Mary MacKillop, are taken from Statement of Mother Mary MacKillop, 23 May 1872, Archives of Propaganda Fide, Rome: SOCG 1873 vol. 1000, 1308-1311. <www.library.unisa.edu.au/condon/CatholicLetters/18720523A.htm> Accessed 15 March 2016. Also from Report and Statement by Sisters Teresa McDonald and Monica Phillips, 25 May, 1872, Archives of Propaganda Fide, Rome: SOCG 1873 vol. 1000, 1304-1307. <www.library.unisa.edu.au/condon/CatholicLetters/18720525A.htm> Accessed 15 March 2016.

14. Bishop Sheil offered the convent to the Dominican Sisters on condition that they took responsibility for the debt owing on it. Thus in Foale's words: '[They] were drawn unwittingly into the conflict about to wrack the Church in the Colony and they suffered a great deal before that conflict was resolved.' Foale, *The Josephite Story*, 91.

as yet untrained or involved in one of the works of charity and some invalids. In spite of Teresa's efforts to protect one of the Sisters who was ill, Horan and Murphy went to the dormitory where she was in bed. Such was the distress caused to the Sisters during the taking of the inventory that Teresa, incensed by the priests' abrasive manner, could not keep silent. She 'reproached them with their unmanly— not to say unpriestly—conduct, accusing them of taking advantage of their [the Sisters'] superior's absence and their helpless condition. In the warmth of her indignation she said that as the forefathers of the Sisters had bled for their faith, so would they now for their Rule.' Then, ignoring Teresa's position as Little Sister, they altered the present arrangements and gave the Sisters new appointments insisting that these be taken up immediately. Knowing that the priests would be offended by her accusations and possibly not wishing to antagonise the bishop, Teresa apologised to them before they left the convent.

While Mary was on her way back to Adelaide, she wrote a letter to Bishop Sheil stating that her first duty was to God and the Rule which she had vowed to follow.[15] If he changed the Rule—which it seemed he had already done—she would have no option but to take up the alternative he offered—to be dispensed of her vows. Greatly displeased by her stance, he ordered Mary to go to Bagot's Gap that evening—an order she was unable to follow for in her words, 'I had not the means to do so.' But that evening in a conversation with Teresa, Horan downplayed the changes to the Rule and told her to assemble the Sisters for a meeting at 10.00 the following morning. He also conveyed a message from Sheil that instead of Bagot's Gap, the bishop wished Mary to go to St John's at Kapunda by the first train in the morning. But this ploy to remove the Sister Guardian from the scene did not succeed. Mary wanted to speak to Sheil himself because she doubted the sincerity of those who spoke to her, and really did not know whom to believe. Early in the evening and after discussion of the whole matter with Teresa who remained with her as a witness, Mary spoke to Horan insisting that she must speak with the bishop before leaving for Kapunda. To his question regarding her intention to go to St John's the next morning, Mary—intent on safeguarding the integrity of the Rule and aware of her responsibility to remain with the Sisters—replied: 'Father, how can I under those rules?' Horan

---

15. MacKillop to Sheil, 10.9.1871.

then left the convent and after Mary had encouraged the Sisters to 'do what they thought would please God most' regarding the new Rule, she retired for the night.

Father Horan did not. Later that evening he returned to the Mother House where he informed Teresa that 'in consequence of Sister Mary's rebellious conduct in not complying with the Bishop's wishes, he [the bishop] had excommunicated her.'[16] As requested by Horan, Teresa took this message to Mary who replied with her own message that she 'could not act but as she had done.' After she had delivered Mary's reply, Teresa took the opportunity to remind the priest that it was not under Mary's influence that the Sisters had confirmed their intention of adhering to the Rule. She also reminded him that he had been told before by other Sisters that they could not conform to the new Rule.

About eight o'clock the following morning (22 September), Bishop Sheil arrived at the convent accompanied by four priests one of whom was Father Horan. When the bishop asked the reason for the Sisters' absence that morning at Mass, Teresa replied that they thought that they were all excommunicated with Sister Mary and therefore it would be inappropriate for them to attend Mass. Both the bishop and Horan accused Teresa of misunderstanding what had been said the night before after which she begged their pardon for having not understood correctly. When some thirty of the Sisters had assembled in the oratory and with Mary kneeling before him, Sheil pronounced the words of excommunication. Teresa immediately moved forward and knelt beside Mary but the bishop ordered her to return to her place. Mary left the oratory at once amid grief and turmoil among the Sisters. Next Sheil proceeded to call out the names of those he had classified as lay Sisters, but they would not accept. When some other Sisters asked for a dispensation from their vows, he refused to give it stating that any Sister who attempted to leave the Institute without his permission would be excommunicated. As the bishop and priests left

---

16. There was some confusion about what Horan actually said. In Teresa's evidence to the Commission on 3 June, 1872 she stated that Horan told her that "Sister Mary was under excommunication if she did not obey the Bishop's wishes with regard to the changes to the Rule." Evidence of Sister Teresa McDonald, 3 June 1872. Archives of Propaganda Fide, Rome: SOCG 1873 vol. 1000, 1394v-1395. <www.library.unisa.edu.au/condon.CatholicLetters/18720603.htm> Accessed 16 March 2016.

the oratory, they removed the Blessed Sacrament from the tabernacle. The entire community left the convent that day.

Mary sought refuge in the home of James Woods, Father Woods' brother. Most of the Sisters moved into the house that had been rented after Sheil's previous direction that they were to leave the Franklin Street convent. Mary had no hesitation in placing her confidence in Teresa's ability to lead the community in such troubled times. As she explained to Woods: 'Sister Teresa must, of course, remain as Little Sister and you know how safe all who are under her will be.'[17] As well as the position of superior, and in obedience to the Bishop she had taken over the Hall school and was occupied there each day. But Sheil, or most likely Horan, had not forgotten the manner in which she had supported Mary on the morning of the excommunication. For showing such 'contempt and disrespect' in kneeling beside Mary, the bishop expelled Teresa from the Institute adding that 'her vows were not extinct until she removed the Habit.' He later accused her of writing a letter which spoke of him in derogatory terms. He then appointed Sister Monica Phillips superior but because his terms and directives were so confused she eventually wrote to Sheil requesting for herself and the Sisters a dispensation from their vows. This was granted. On 20 October Horan called at the Hall school to inform the Sisters that they were to finish up at the school that day and deposit the key with him.

When word of the Sisters' difficulties reached Emanuel Solomon, an Adelaide Jew and staunch friend of the Institute, he offered them one of his houses rent free for as long as they needed it. By the end of October some twenty Sisters, out of the habit, were settled there with Sister Teresa as Little Sister. They divided their time between work, study and prayer with a few of the Sisters going out to work. Three women were received as externs.[18] Circumstances prevented the establishment of a foundation in the Bathurst diocese, as Bishop Quinn had requested, but five Sisters left for Queensland in late January 1872.[19] In the meantime, some sixty Sisters—numbering over

---

17. MacKillop to Woods:19.12.1871.
18. MacKillop to Woods, 26.10.1871.
19. MacKillop to Woods, 22.1.1872.

half the Institute, faithful to the Rule and still wearing their habits—remained at their posts.[20]

But although the Sisters were making the best of their circumstances, holding fast to the Rule and carrying on their work wherever possible, the situation in which they had been placed meant that they all lived in a state of anxiety and uncertainty.[21] With the life and Rule they had chosen under threat, their superior placed under the severe sanction of excommunication, owning no property, totally dependent for their livelihood on the charity of others and the destruction of their Institute still the object of Horan and his colleagues, they suffered. Only their trust in God held any hope for the future. While Father Woods 'suffered a great deal' due to his absence from the Sisters for whom he was deeply concerned, he seemed to lack an understanding of the gravity of their situation.[22] Thus he pressed Mary and the novice mistress, Monica Phillips, to leave Adelaide for the Bathurst diocese in order to establish a foundation.[23] His continued support of the visionaries increased the already heavy burden Mary carried.[24] For her part, Mary carried out her duties with the support of many people, in particular the Jesuit Fathers. Irrespective of her own personal position, she faced the situation with unbounded faith and hope, unflinching resolve and abiding charity.

As the year gradually drew to its conclusion, Teresa continued to serve as Little Sister of the community living in the house so generously made available to the Institute. In November at Mary MacKillop's insistence, she spent a week resting at Gawler. Just prior to Christmas she visited her parents who were ill. On her return she went to take charge of the novices at Norwood where they had been sent to be under the care of the Jesuit Fathers. The New Year saw her busy accompanying Sisters to their various destinations.[25]

The New Year also brought a marked decline in the bishop's health. After the news of Mary MacKillop's excommunication had appeared in the press and public sentiment had been aroused, Sheil

---

20. Foale, *The Josephite Story*, 101.
21. MacKillop to Woods, 8.10.1871.
22. Woods to MacKillop, 29.9.1871; 10.10.1871.
23. Woods to MacKillop, 29.9.1871; 2.1.1872.
24. MacKillop to Woods, 22.1.1872; 14.2.1872.
25. MacKillop to Woods, 7.11.71; 23.12.71; 23.3.1872.

had become somewhat restrained in his demands on the Sisters. Even prior to Christmas Mary was reporting to Woods that 'the poor Bishop seems strangely altered. He is very rarely at West Terrace and has been very ill of late.'[26] In fact he moved out to one of the country parishes, Willunga, where before his death on 1 March 1872 he appointed Father Christopher Reynolds to be administrator of the diocese. Also prior to his death, he sent for Mary MacKillop but on her way to see him she was met by Father Hughes who, in the Bishop's name unconditionally removed the excommunication. One of Father Reynolds' first actions was to reappoint Mary MacKillop to her position of Sister Guardian of the Institute and to re-admit those who, due to circumstances beyond their control, had left the Institute. Then, some three weeks later, the Sisters renewed their vows. It was also at this time that Teresa made her life vows.[27]

Throughout the entire Josephite affair the newspapers had carried both support and condemnation of the Institute and Bishop Sheil. This intensified after the reinstatement of Mary MacKillop and the Sisters as Horan and his colleagues continued to pursue the suppression of the Institute. After a civil law suit against one of the newspapers cleared the Sisters' names and convicted the editor of criminal libel, the matter gradually settled. Father Horan and his close supporter, Father Nowlan, were eventually dismissed from the diocese. However, prior to Christmas 1871, some Catholic laymen had informed Rome of affairs in the Adelaide diocese and asked that an official inquiry be established. The Roman authorities took action so that on 23 May 1872 Father Reynolds wrote that the Bishops of Hobartown and Bathurst were soon expected in Adelaide where they would conduct an official ecclesiastical inquiry into the case of the Sisters of St Joseph and the state of the diocese.[28]

The Apostolic Commissioners, Bishops Murphy of Hobart and Quinn of Bathurst began the inquiry on 1 June. Mary MacKillop and a number of Sisters, including Teresa McDonald, were questioned.

26. MacKillop to Woods, 19.12.1871.
27. MacKillop to Flora MacKillop, 26.2.1872; MacKillop to Woods, 23.3.1872. Reynold to Cardinal Barnabo, Prefect of the Congregation of Propaganda Fide, 23.5.1872. Archives of Propaganda Fide, Rome: SOCG 1873 vol.1000 1317-1323. <www.library.unisa.edu.au/condon/Catholic Letters/18720523B htm> Accessed 19 March 2016.
28. Reynolds to Cardinal Barnabo, 23.5.1872.

Father Woods was also required to give evidence, as were several other priests.[29] At the conclusion of the proceedings, the two bishops sent a report of their findings to Rome. While the central part that Bishop Sheil had played in the troubles in Adelaide during his episcopate was not acknowledged, the Commissioners recommended that Horan and Nowlan, whom they judged to have caused the troubles, be recalled to their monasteries. Regarding Father Woods, they recommended he be relieved of all responsibility for the Sisters of St Joseph and the Institute. Father Tappeiner was to continue as Spiritual Director of the Institute. While they recommended that the Josephite Rule be revised by competent ecclesiastical authority, they praised Mary MacKillop and the Sisters for their admirable conduct throughout all the troubles.[30]

And so, after the turmoil, confusion, hardship and suffering of the previous months, the Josephites were left to continue their lives according to the original Rule and to carry on their work in the schools and institutions.

The Sister Guardian had no doubt of the part Teresa had played in holding together and supporting the Institute during the times when she was absent from Adelaide.

> Sister Teresa acted beautifully whilst I was away. She was like a broken-hearted yet spirited Mother trying to save her children, and in the heat of the moment spoke words which made Father Horan throw down his pen and say that he could not go on. But she did all in such a beautiful way that they not only respected her the more, and seemed afraid to question

---

29. Final Report of the Apostolic Commissioners Daniel Murphy (Bishop of Hobart-town) and Matthew Quinn (Bishop of Bathurst). 10 July 1872. Archives of Propaganda Fide, Rome: SOCG 1873 vol.1000 1359-1377v. <www.library. unisa.edu.au/condon/CatholicLetters/18720710.htm> Accessed 9 March 2016. Evidence of Sister Teresa MacDonald.3 June 1872. The Evidence of Father Julian E. Tenison Woods, 28 June 1872, Archives of Propaganda Fide, Rome: SOCG: 1873 vol.1000, 1422-1424. <www.library.unisa.edu.au/condon/ CatholicLetters/18720628.htm> Accessed 1 March 2016.

30. Father Woods finally left Adelaide on 8 August 1872. The visionaries all left the Institute in 1872 except Helena Myles who was a member of the second group of Sisters to go to the Bathurst diocese in 1873, returned to Adelaide in 1876 and finally left the Institute in 1879.

her in any way. Indeed, dear Father, we have a priceless treasure in that Sister.[31]

The harsh words of Father Horan did not intimidate Teresa, nor did his efforts to mislead her succeed. Spirited and ready to defend her Sisters she had stood up to the priest and in dealing with the bishop acted in a firm but courteous manner. It was to Teresa's care that Mary entrusted the displaced Sisters after they had been ordered to leave the Mother House. It was from Teresa that Mary sought advice in moments of uncertainty and it was Teresa she chose when sensitive conversations required a witness. It was during the excommunication that Teresa most showed her mettle, kneeling beside Mary in a gesture of loyalty and solidarity. Expelled from the Institute for her actions and wrongly accused of defaming the bishop in a letter, she remained in Mary's words 'humble but firm,' indeed 'a priceless treasure.'[32]

It was no wonder then that Teresa's name came into consideration in regard to future foundations of the Institute. Bishop Matthew Quinn had asked for a foundation of Sisters in the Bathurst diocese in 1871. He had repeated that invitation at the height of the Institute's troubles.[33] During the early months of 1872, Mary and Father Woods had exchanged views on which Sisters might be suitable for the Bathurst diocese.[34] With the presence of Bishop Quinn in Adelaide in June for the Commission and a repeated invitation, the matter became more immediate. Woods was in no doubt as to who should lead the founding Sisters: 'I want Sister Teresa . . . to have charge of the Bathurst province.'[35]

Mary, aware of Teresa's ill health, also knew the value of her presence among the Sisters chosen for the venture. At first she thought of sending Sister Calasanctius Howley as a support for Teresa:

> I will keep Sisters Teresa and Calasanctius at any rate free until I hear from you, for should any have to go to Bathurst, I think it would require those two to be of the number, Sister Teresa not being well enough able either for the school or to

---

31. MacKillop to Woods, 19.9.1872.
32. MacKillop to Woods, 16.11.1871; MacKillop to Woods; 26.9.1871.
33. Woods to MacKillop, 20.9.1871; 29.9.1871' 2.1.1872.
34. MacKillop to Woods, 22.1.1872; 19.2.1872; 5.3.1872.
35. Woods to MacKillop, 16.2.1872.

teach the Sisters who may be with her. But her knowledge of the spirit of the Rule is beautiful, and with her in Bathurst I think all would be well.[36]

But when the final group was chosen, Calasanctius was not among its number. Teresa McDonald was named as Little Sister and Provincial of the first Josephite foundation in New South Wales. The child who had made the voyage from Scotland to Australia, and the young woman who had sailed from Perth to Adelaide, now as a mature Josephite woman prepared for yet another journey. Her destination was Queen Charlotte Vale—a tiny settlement near Bathurst, New South Wales.

Teresa of the Incarnat.

---

36. MacKillop to Woods, 23.3.1872.

11
Journey To The Vale

After the intensity of the Commission of Inquiry and the relief at its conclusion, Teresa had little time to prepare for departure on the coastal steamer *Rangatira* scheduled to leave Port Adelaide on 4 July 1872 bound for Melbourne and Sydney. As were the other members of the founding community to The Vale, she was leaving her parents and family. Just prior to Christmas when her parents had been ill, Teresa had visited them. Moving so far away would be a hardship for them and for her. She relied on Mary MacKillop to soften the blow of her departure: 'I hope you wrote home to my poor parents who must think me very cold hearted.'[1]

The other members of the group were also leaving their families.

The Irish-born Sister Joseph Dwyer had come to Adelaide with her parents as a small child.[2] She had joined the Institute in 1868. Being stationed at some distance from Adelaide, she had avoided the immediate repercussions of the excommunication maintaining her religious habit and continuing to observe the Rule. A little over a month prior to leaving for The Vale, she made her life vows as a Sister of St Joseph. An astute, intelligent and well-educated woman, Joseph was to prove a rock of strength to Teresa throughout their time in the Bathurst diocese.

---

1. McDonald to MacKillop, 8.7.1872.
2. Mary Dwyer (Sister Joseph of the Holy Family) was born on 18.5. 1850. She came to Adelaide with her parents, Denis Dwyer and Catherine Power, in 1854. She joined the Institute in February, 1868 and spent over three years in the Bathurst diocese before returning to Adelaide in 1876. She later returned to New South Wales where she served for a time as Provincial in Sydney. She died in Sydney in 1937.

Sister Hyacinth Quinlan, who also joined the Institute in 1868, was the only Australian-born member of the founding group.[3] After enduring the disturbance of the excommunication, she joined with her Sisters in officially resuming the religious life in March 1872. It was not until the conclusion of the first retreat conducted by Father Woods at The Vale in December 1872, that Hyacinth made her life vows. A crucial decision made by Hyacinth in January 1876 resulted in her complete break from the Sisters of St Joseph under the authority of Mary MacKillop. As a Sister of St Joseph under episcopal authority she served for fifty-seven years in three dioceses.[4]

The fourth member of the community was a young lay woman, Ada Braham, who had emigrated from England to South Australia with her Jewish parents. Following a close association with Mary MacKillop and Father Woods, Ada was received into the Catholic Church taking the name Mary Joseph. She had gone to Queensland with Mary MacKillop in December 1869. There she proved to be a source of much severe disruption and anxiety for the community but after returning to Adelaide in 1871 where she received some treatment, she gradually settled.[5] During the following months she developed a strong dependency on Teresa so that when word went around that Teresa might be appointed to The Vale, Mary Joseph begged to be allowed to accompany her. In a pleading letter to Father Woods she wrote: '. . . if you send my darling Sister Teresa to Bathurst without me I'm sure my heart will quite break.'[6] Eventually she was included in the group as a prospective postulant. Later, at The Vale, she was formally received into the Institute as Sister Aloysius and made her first vows as a Sister of St Joseph.[7]

---

3. Bridget Quinlan (Sister Hyacinth of St John the Baptist) was born in the Clare district of South Australia on 20.8.1850 of Irish parents Richard Quinlan and Lucy Naulty. She joined the Institute on 16.8.1868 and after a time in the Bathurst diocese moved to the diocesan Josephite foundations in New Zealand and later Tasmania where she died in 1933.
4. For more information on this decision and its repercussions see Crowley, *Women of The Vale*, Chapter 3.
5. Woods to MacKillop, 5.7.1870.
6. Braham to Woods, 8.9.1871.
7. Ada Braham (Sister Aloysius of Our Lady of Dolours) was born in London on 7.9.1854. Her parents were Benjamin Braham and Ada Solomon who after their arrival in South Australia settled in the Portland/Penola area. She formally joined the Institute on 1.11.1872. After Teresa's death she moved to Adelaide

Given Teresa's record of ill health, Mary and Father Woods' choice to send her on such a distant and for the most part unknown mission was surprising since both were fully aware of her health problems. That they did decide on her to lead the foundation, bears witness to her standing with the co-founders. They knew her worth as a Sister of St Joseph and trusted her ability to establish a firm Josephite foundation. As a novice in Kapunda and Penola she had shown a deep capacity to know and live out the spirit of the young Australian Institute. She had come out of her Adelaide experience well-tried in adversity and somewhat battle-worn. But how well prepared was Teresa for the Bathurst mission? Her knowledge of the Bishop of Bathurst, Matthew Quinn, was confined to his participation in the Commission of Inquiry where he had treated the Sisters 'in the kindest possible manner.'[8] Yet did either or both of the co-founders warn her that, months prior to the Commission, Bishop Quinn had stated that 'the Sisters were no more than a diocesan congregation,' and had hinted to Woods that 'there would be no central government?'[9] Teresa had good reason to be well aware of the tumultuous repercussions of the South Australian clerical efforts to destroy the central government of the Institute. That experience alone would have put her on her guard as she moved into another diocese. Knowledge of what Quinn seemed to be thinking and planning—if she were party to that knowledge—at the least would have increased her level of vigilance, if not raised alarm. There was also Teresa's experience of Father Woods who she knew planned to follow the Sisters to the Bathurst diocese as soon as possible. She had observed his lack of discernment and common sense as he fell under the spell of the visionaries. Frustrated by his gullibility she had admitted to Mary 'awful repugnant feelings and dislikes' towards the Father Director.[10] Although the Commission had recommended that Woods be relieved of all responsibility for the Sisters of St Joseph and

---

for a short time but later returned to the Bathurst diocese. She died at The Vale on 21.3.1877 and was buried next to Teresa in the cemetery beside the convent. For information regarding Mary Joseph in Queensland see Margaret McKenna, *With Joyful Hearts! Mary MacKillop and the Sisters of St Joseph in Queensland 1870–1970* (Sydney: Sisters of St Joseph, 2009), 109–110. Crowley, *Women of The Vale*, 27–28.

8. MacKillop to Woods 4.6.1872.
9. Quinn to Woods 12.1.1873.
10. McDonald to MacKillop, 3.7.1870.

the Institute, Teresa might well have suspected that, once he was far removed from Adelaide, he would ignore that directive and, in a new location and in a newly-formed community, resume his former role of Spiritual Director.

Whatever her apprehension or premonitions regarding the mission to the Bathurst Diocese, Teresa would have been cheered by the company of two women who had shared the Josephite life with her for some four years. Although at thirty-three Teresa was twelve years their senior, both Joseph Dwyer and Hyacinth Quinlan at twenty-one years of age had experienced the challenges of religious life and established themselves as teachers. Most importantly, all three had been instructed by the co-founders in the religious life and in particular in the spirit and practice of the Josephite Rule. At various times each had shared community life with Mary MacKillop, absorbing her spirit of prayerfulness and her humility, poverty and charity. Each had thrown in her lot with the first women who gathered as Sisters of St Joseph before the group had received any official recognition or status. They had shared the early days of struggle, working long and hard in isolated settlements in South Australia. During the confusion and uncertainty of the previous months, they had proved themselves staunch followers of the Josephite Rule. And each Sister held the memory of those recent events that told of a fragile and vulnerable Institute—memories that ensured watchfulness and caution in the days ahead. Indeed, these three Sisters had much to offer in meeting the challenge of establishing a Josephite foundation in the Bathurst diocese.

While there remains no extant material indicating how Teresa, Joseph and Hyacinth felt about the inclusion of the 18-year-old Mary Joseph in their group, speculation suggests that they might have held some reservations. All three knew of the trouble she had caused as part of the founding group in Brisbane. Once away from Adelaide as part of another founding group, would she revert to her former ways? Or would the degree of recovery which she had shown after her return to Adelaide continue? Teresa, in particular, could well have worried about her own situation in regard to Mary Joseph. Would the young woman's dependency on her develop into something akin to Rose's illness? In the event of that happening, would the Provincial, herself far from well, have the strength to cope? Whatever of their possible uneasiness, the Sisters also knew that Mary Joseph had remained with the Institute through the difficult months of the excommunication and had 'shared all their poverty willingly and cheerfully.'[11] In her own way she too knew what it meant to be a Sister of St Joseph.

It was with mixed feelings then that the four women bound for The Vale boarded the *Rangatira* at Port Adelaide on 4 July 1872. With only a three-hour stop at Port Melbourne, the steamer made a speedy passage to Sydney. That was fortunate as Teresa reported to Mary that they were 'very sea sick' and that Mary Joseph never left her bunk during the entire voyage.[12] Once on land they made their way to Mrs Casey's private lodging house. So crowded was the establishment that only two beds were available for the Sisters. As she and Sister Joseph sat up through the night Teresa, 'still sea sick,' assured the Sister Guardian back in Adelaide that 'we are very happy and contented.'[13] The following morning Teresa contacted Father Joly, one of the Marist priests who had provided friendship and assistance to both Father Woods and also to Mary MacKillop and the community on their way to Brisbane. He arranged accommodation for Teresa and the Sisters with the Benedictine nuns whose monastery, Subiaco, was located in the Marist parish. The warm welcome extended to them by the nuns was deeply appreciated by the Josephites who felt rather lonely so far from home.[14]

The few days spent in Sydney were busy. Teresa interviewed three prospective postulants who were hoping to meet with Father Woods before setting out for Adelaide. The Sisters and Mary Joseph visited the Marist house, Villa Maria. Their meetings with the Sisters were significant in that they provided the Josephites with their first encounter with women religious of congregations other than their own. Teresa recounted how edified and comforted they were when the Benedictines sang the Office, when they shared recreation with their hosts and when the Benedictine superior promised to help

---

11. Sister Mechtilde Woods, 'History of the Sisters of St Joseph', unpublished, 1918, 43. An indication of Teresa's doubts about including Mary Joseph in The Vale community might be gained by Mechtilde Woods' comment: 'Sr Teresa consented although she knew that Ada Braham [Mary Joseph] would be a trial to her.' Mechtilde Woods, 'History', 85.
12. McDonald to MacKillop, 8.7.1872.
13. McDonald to MacKillop, 8.7.1872.
14. McDonald to MacKillop, 8.7.1872.

them in any way possible. The Marist priests also encouraged the new arrivals as did Archbishop Polding who, during a meeting with the Josephites, 'gave . . . a nice little exhortation.'[15] These were important meetings for Teresa and her Sisters who, far from home and with the unsettling memory of the previous months still fresh, were assured that they were not without friends in New South Wales.

Thus heartened on their way, The Vale community made plans to travel by train to Macquarie Plains as instructed by Father McAuliffe.[16] When Teresa found that she did not have enough money for the train fares, the Mother Superior lent her the necessary amount. With the tickets in hand, and some food as well as a case of oranges generously supplied by the Benedictines, the little group left Sydney on Saturday 13 July. Teresa later described the eight-hour journey as 'a most dreary road.'[17] They were delighted therefore to be met by Father McAuliffe with Bishop Quinn's travelling coach waiting to take them to Bathurst where they would stay with the Sisters of Mercy.

The Josephites were overwhelmed by the warmth and friendship of the Mercy Sisters who, well aware of the ordeals of Adelaide, called them 'St Joseph's persecuted Sisters.' Teresa found the formality of the convent somewhat different from the Josephite way. After each Sister was shown to her bedroom, high tea in honour of the visitors was taken by the entire community. Sitting next to the Mother Superior, Teresa was concerned that Mary Joseph—at the far end of the table— would conduct herself appropriately. But she need not have worried as her young charge, surrounded by Mercy Sisters, excelled herself in every way.[18]

The next morning the Josephites set out with Father McAuliffe for their new home. Situated some 10 kilometres from Bathurst, The

---

15. McDonald to MacKillop, 8.7.1872. McDonald to MacKillop, 23.7.1872. Quinlan to Walsh, 19.7.1872.
16. Macquarie Plains railway station, later named Brewongle station, was located on the western line a few kilometres east of Bathurst. It would not be until four years after the Sisters' arrival at The Vale that the construction of the line would be completed as far as Bathurst. Father John McAuliffe was the administrator of the Catholic parish of Bathurst. He organised the Sisters' journey from Sydney because Bishop Matthew Quinn, who was travelling overland from Adelaide, had not yet returned to Bathurst.
17. McDonald to MacKillop, 23.7.1872.
18. McDonald to McKillop, 23.7.1872.

Vale village consisted of 'scarcely a dozen houses.'[19] It was the dead of winter and even Father McAuliffe—who had previous experience of the seasons in Bathurst—commented on 'the cold and misery of the place.'[20] Although the construction of the convent had begun, there was no place for the Sisters to live and begin their work apart from the little slab church which offered no protection against the harsh wind and cold.[21] Aware of these tough conditions the Sisters of Mercy and Father McAuliffe offered accommodation in the convent and presbytery in Bathurst. The Josephites, however, had different ideas. Founded to live and work in the isolation, poverty and hardship of Australia, they decided to move immediately out to The Vale—or as Teresa called it 'our own little place.'[22]

Once that decision was made, there was a flurry of activity to prepare the basic necessities for the Sisters. Father McAuliffe procured four beds. The Sisters of Mercy made the mattresses and provided a length of damask needed to screen off that portion of the church which was to serve as a dormitory. They also packed a supply of tea, sugar, meat and bread for the Josephites. Father McAuliffe, who saw to the removal of all these goods to The Vale, also alerted the village people of the arrival of the Sisters.

Teresa wrote a graphic description of their arrival at The Vale on 16 July 1872:

> At 2 o'clock Fr McAuliffe called for us in the grand carriage on the feast of Mount Carmel and away we went . . . The people and children were there to meet us, took off their hats, clapped their hands and cried hurrah . . . Fr McAuliffe had lollies and cakes for the children that were there. The people were so glad and in the evening came with eatables and other things. We had no sheets and Fr McAuliffe was in such a way a

---

19. Braham to MacKillop, 23.11.1872.
20. McDonald to MacKillop, 23.7.1872.
21. This church was located just south of the present convent building at Perthville. In 1886, when St John's brick Church was erected, the slab church was taken down and re-erected close to the new church. It was used as a primary and infants' school until 1956 when it was demolished to make way for four new classrooms.
22. McDonald to MacKillop, 23.7.1872.

woman promised to bring some. He watched everything and
saw everything done by men who came for the purpose.[23]

So concerned was the priest for the Sisters' welfare that he returned
the following morning convinced that after one night in the church
they would seek the relative comfort of Bathurst. Seeing they were
settled and after giving some directives regarding bed coverings,
eating meat twice a day and not rising at five o'clock in the mornings,
he returned to Bathurst.

Though appreciative of the welcome and care of the Sisters of
Mercy, Father McAuliffe and The Vale people, Teresa and her Sisters
keenly felt the isolation of their new home and were lonely for the
Mother House. 'This is a bush place,' she wrote to Mary MacKillop,
'we can get nothing . . . we have not had one line from anyone since
we left.' Nonetheless, they were in their 'own little place' and looked
ahead to the challenge of the new foundation.

---

23. McDonald to MacKillop, 23.7.1872.

12

Our Own Little Place

For more than 40,000 years prior to the arrival of the Sisters of St Joseph at The Vale, the Wiradjuri people had lived on the land and along the river which later would be named the Macquarie. It was not until after the barrier of the Great Dividing Range had been crossed in 1813, that the of New South Wales Governor, Lachlan Macquarie and his wife had travelled the newly-completed road over the Divide. On the banks of the river that already bore his name, Macquarie proclaimed the town of Bathurst. A few days later the official party explored to the south west of the town naming the creek in the area Queen Charlotte Vale.[1] The gathering of huts and make-do houses that had sprung up along its banks some 10 kilometres from Bathurst was given the same name—later abbreviated to The Vale.[2]

For many years the road on which the Macquaries travelled was the only access from Sydney to the interior of the Colony. Consequently Bathurst, which provided a resting place and the opportunity for simple supplies, gradually developed. It was not until the 1850s that the town and surrounds saw a remarkable movement of men, women and children in search of fortune on the newly-discovered goldfields. As they moved out into the western area of the Colony more towns sprang up. Later, when the gold reserves were exhausted, the towns remained as service centres for those who sought their living as pastoralists or in a trade or profession.

---

1. Queen Charlotte was the wife of King George 111, the British sovereign at that time.
2. At some later date the village was renamed Perth after Perth in Scotland the birthplace of Sir George Murray the Secretary of State for War and the Colonies at that time. Confusion with Perth, Western Australia, caused that name to be changed to Perthville in 1908.

The archbishop of Sydney, John Polding, whose diocese included the towns and settlements west of the Great Divide, appointed the first resident priests to Bathurst in 1838. By 1864 the number of priests had increased, and certified Catholic denominational schools had been established in Bathurst, Orange, Mudgee, Wellington and Sofala.[3] But while these provided spiritual care and instruction in the more closely-settled areas, Catholics in the outlying regions were visited by a priest only a few times a year. It was to meet the needs of these isolated Catholics and to facilitate the administration of such a vast area that Rome formally established the Diocese of Bathurst on 20 June 1865. Stretching from Bathurst to the borders of Queensland, South Australia and Victoria and with a scattered Catholic population of 13,000, it was a diocese which held many challenges.

The man appointed as bishop of the vast diocese was Matthew Quinn. Born in Ireland in 1821, Matthew grew up surrounded by the poverty and struggle of his nation. Such an environment was partly responsible for the fighting spirit and relentless defence of the Catholic Church which characterised Quinn's entire life. As a boy he absorbed the thinking of a male-dominated society and accepted the unchallenged power and control exercised by the Catholic clergy. These attitudes were confirmed during his priestly formation in Rome which he began at the age of sixteen.

After his ordination in 1845, Matthew volunteered for missionary work in India. When his health broke down seven years later, he returned to Ireland where he worked with his brother, Father James Quinn, at the seminary of St Lawrence O'Toole in Dublin. When James was appointed bishop of Brisbane in 1859, Matthew took on his position of president of the seminary. He was still in that position when he received his episcopal appointment. After arriving in Bathurst in 1866 he was installed as the first bishop of the newly-established diocese on 1 November of that year. A year later, after he had time to come to grips with the challenges he faced, Quinn wrote

---

3. A dual system of education had existed in NSW since 1848. The Board of National Education administered the government schools while the Denominational School Board administered the denominational schools. Certified denominational schools were Church schools supervised by local boards under the authority of the Denominational School Board and assisted by a government subsidy provided they were certified.

to a friend in Ireland: 'The cares of my weighty position multiply and press upon me. The thoughts of the length and breadth, the roughness and toughness of this diocese often overwhelm me.'[4]

The year 1866 stands out as a significant one in the history of the Catholic Church in Australia for three reasons. Firstly, it was in that year that the Institute of the Sisters of St Joseph of the Sacred Heart was founded. Secondly, that year saw the arrival of Bishop Matthew Quinn to the diocese of Bathurst. Thirdly, it was that year which saw the introduction of the Public Schools Act in New South Wales. An Act which established a council of education to administer all schools in the Colony, its passing was highly significant for Catholic denominational schools because it took away certain elements of autonomy previously enjoyed by those schools. In short, it established an education system which would qualify to receive State funding only if it were secular and which would be controlled by a council over which Catholic authorities had no control.

The newly-arrived bishop immediately mounted a crusade against the Act but soon realised he would not succeed. Then, supported by the bishops of Maitland and Goulburn, he announced that the Catholic Church in New South Wales would establish its own education system independent of the State. Quinn knew that to make this plan work, he would need skilled teachers to staff these schools. He also knew that the diocese had no money either to train or pay the teachers. But he was also aware of the Sisters of St Joseph founded to live and teach in the most isolated towns and rural areas of Australia. Bishop Quinn first heard of these Sisters through Bishop Sheil and Father Woods whom he met at the provincial synod of bishops in Melbourne in 1869. He first met the Sisters while on a visit to Adelaide in 1871 and a year later during the Commission of Inquiry. But even prior to that, he had decided not only to invite them to the diocese, but to stipulate the location of the first foundation. 'The foundation at Bathurst is chosen—a poor little school at Vale Road five miles from Bathurst. The Sacristy will be your convent at first, so

---

4. Quinn to a Sister, 30.12.1867. DBA. Among the problems faced by Quinn were a £4,000 debt on the church in Bathurst, the doubtful quality and calibre of some priests of the diocese and the inadequate training and questionable dedication of most of the teachers who staffed denominational schools which were poorly resourced and generally run down.

we shall begin well . . .'[5] Quinn was convinced that the Sisters of St Joseph—a workforce which would require no salary and over which he would establish his control—were just the women he needed to meet the challenges of Catholic education in his diocese.

The relationship of three significant events of 1866—the founding of the Sisters of St Joseph, the arrival of Bishop Matthew Quinn to the diocese of Bathurst and the passing of the Education Act—formed the context of the foundation made at The Vale. They were the backdrop against which Teresa and her Sisters arrived at their new home on that cold July morning in 1872.

The winter of 1872 went down in the memory of the Bathurst people as 'the coldest that had been known for many years.'[6] Thick frost lay on the ground at The Vale, icy winds whistled through the cracks of the slab church and a heavy fall of snow in August covered the entire village and surrounding hills. The Sisters' only supply of water was stored in an outside cask. Often it would be covered with ice which had to be broken with a hammer before any water became available. Their only comfort was the fireplace in the sacristy where they kept a fire burning day and night. There they cooked in a camp oven, ate their meals and gathered for some warmth. Teresa, whose childhood memory of Scottish winters had grown dim, summed up her experience: 'This place is most awfully cold . . . when we are dressing ourselves in the morning our clothes seem frozen and we ourselves frozen also.'[7] But irrespective of the living conditions Teresa was able to assure Mary: 'We are all very good and keep Rule pretty well under the circumstances.'[8]

The cold of that first winter was in sharp contrast to the warmth of friendship and support given to the community by the village people. They kept up a ready supply of water, of chopped wood for the fire

---

5. Woods to MacKillop, 19.4.1872.
6. Sister de Sales Tobin, 'History of the Bathurst Foundation', unpublished, Adelaide: 1883, 1. Anne Tobin (Sister de Sales) was born in Tambaroora where her father was a miner. She was the teacher at the Catholic denominational school at The Vale prior to the Sisters' arrival. She joined the Institute on 9 January 1873. After going to Adelaide at the time of the separation, she wrote a short history of the foundation at The Vale.
7. McDonald to MacKillop, 23.7.1872.
8. McDonald to MacKillop, 23.7.1872.

and '[gave] the Sisters almost everything they needed.'[9] Teresa, who 'endeared herself to all by her gentleness and kindliness of manner,' was soon a favourite with the people. 'They thought of nothing but pleasing her and ministering to her comfort and that of her Sisters.'[10] Father McAuliffe, whom Bishop Quinn appointed the Sisters' confessor, also took a lively interest in the welfare of the community.

On the day of the Sisters' arrival at The Vale, Teresa had told the twenty-four assembled school children that the Sisters would commence teaching on the following Monday, 22 July. However, she spent part of the week prior to that classifying the children, allocating classes to the Sisters and, after examining the text books, placing an order to Adelaide for books authorised for use in Catholic schools. Mary Joseph was given charge of the twelve first class children, Sister Joseph the second class and Sister Hyacinth the third class. While part of the church remained screened off as the Sisters' dormitory, the rest of the building continued to be used for classes and for the celebration of Mass at 10 am every Sunday and on some weekdays.

From the first day of class, the Sisters operated the school and taught lessons in keeping with the programmes and system devised for Josephite schools. Products of their time and religious backgrounds, Mary and Father Woods believed that children of poor families required a schooling that would enable them to function within their particular religious, social and economic circumstances. Instruction in Catholic Church teaching, reading, writing and arithmetic held priority. To these were added needlework for the girls and bookkeeping for the boys. Religious instruction was given through the catechism, the popular devotions of the day and the celebration of the sacraments. The weekly timetable was tightly structured. Monday to Thursday was given to explanation and teaching to ensure the children's understanding. This was reinforced by rote answers put to them by the teacher. Friday was a day of review and revision. At the conclusion of lessons the Sisters walked the children home. On the first day of school 30 children arrived, and the Sisters happily settled into work.

---

9. Tobin, 'History', 2.
10. Tobin, 'History', 2.

One of the first entries in The Vale Diary records Bishop Quinn's initial visit to the community.[11] The entry for Tuesday 23 July reads:

> After school this afternoon His Lordship, accompanied by Fr McAuliffe, paid us a visit. Dr Quinn was very pleased with our little temporary dwelling and said it was the nicest little place he had seen. He gave us his blessing and promised to come often during school time to see our system of teaching.[12]

The bishop was as good as his word because on the following Monday he returned to hear the third class pupils read. His kindly manner in the classroom set the children and the Sisters at ease. 'We all felt so happy while he was with us, and did not feel a bit afraid to teach before him,' Joseph later wrote.[13] Of course, he was not a stranger to any of the Sisters or to the inner workings of the Institute, having served on the Commission of Inquiry in Adelaide just weeks before. He was especially concerned about how the Sisters were coping with the cold in the early morning and told them not to rise until after six—apparently without consultation regarding this change to the timetable. Five days later the bishop paid another visit.[14] He was well-placed therefore to provide Mary MacKillop with an account of the community. Though they were 'not as yet as comfortably [housed] as I would wish,' he wrote, 'they are doing very well here.' In the same letter he told her of his decision 'to make the place where they are at present . . . the Mother House.' Being so close to Bathurst ensured that the Mass and the sacraments would be readily available. Bishop Quinn, however, may have had more on his mind: in ominous words he added: 'Thus they will be always under my own immediate supervision.'[15]

---

11. From the time of the first foundation from the Mother House, Mary and Father Woods insisted that every convent keep a diary that would be sent to Mary at the end of each month. Recording for the most part the Sisters' observance of the Rule, it allowed Mary to offer guidance in her letters. Sister Joseph kept The Vale Diary (1872–1875). For the purpose of this work that diary is referred to as Diary.
12. Diary, 23.7.1872.
13. Diary, 29.7.1872.
14. Diary, 1.8.1872.
15. Quinn to MacKillop, 31.7.1872.

An even more frequent visitor was Father McAuliffe often accompanied by a visiting priest. Knowing that the Sisters had no way of travelling to Bathurst, he served as their messenger and their source of news. All their mail was sent to the bishop's house and delivered to them by Father McAuliffe who also posted outgoing letters. Soon familiar with handwriting, he would sometimes comment on the senders and on one occasion kept a letter, written by Mary to the Sisters, until after Mass 'as nice fast.'[16] To modern ears the attitude of these two clerics towards the Sisters and their dealings with them were paternalistic and intrusive. But isolated from shops and post office, the Sisters needed assistance if they were to live at The Vale. They were also products of contemporary societal and ecclesiastical structures. Whatever their private thoughts may have been, they deeply appreciated the care and generosity provided by both Bishop Quinn and Father McAuliffe.[17]

From their first days at The Vale, Teresa and her Sisters sought to carry out the prescriptions of the Rule and to continue the Josephite traditions in spite of the inconvenience of their living arrangements. Within weeks of their arrival they spent a few days on retreat directed by the Marist priest, Father Monnier.[18] The Diary records their faithfulness to meditation, the rosary, the dolour rosary, spiritual reading and prayers in choir. They had been at The Vale just over a week when they began to visit the families in the village.[19] Hearing of a poor woman who was desperately in need, Teresa and Hyacinth (and on another day Teresa and Joseph) walked the two miles to her house.[20] Catechism classes were conducted every Sunday afternoon for the children and—as specifically directed by Father McAuliffe— for 'the grown up women.'[21] The household tasks were shared equally in the community and on occasions Teresa would take classes to free another Sister to attend to other duties. On the cold winter evenings they 'had recreation sitting together by the fire.'[22] Later, after the

---

16. Diary, 15.8.1872.
17. Quinlan to Walsh, 19.7.1872; Braham to MacKillop, 17.7.1872; Dwyer to MacKillop, 29.9.1872; McDonald to MacKillop, 23.7.1872; 26.11.1872.
18. McDonald to MacKillop, 21.8.1872.
19. Diary, 24.7.1872. 2.8.72.
20. Diary, 4.8.1872; 5.8.1872.
21. Diary, 17.11.1872.
22. Diary, 1.8.72.

weather had improved, they went for walks around the hills—'a very pretty place.'[23] One such walk held a special place in Sister Joseph's memory:

> In the afternoon we went for a little walk up the hills around the convent. Everything seemed so calm and still today. If we had the spirit of contemplation we could soon become contemplatives. As the shades of evening fall nothing is to be heard but the tinkling of the sheep bells and nothing to be seen but the hills, all around peak after peak.[24]

Another of their pastimes was to keep a check on the progress of the convent under construction near the church. As the brickwork neared completion, they prepared a large green flag which bore representations of a cross, an Irish harp, a rose thistle and a shamrock. On the day the work was finally finished, the workmen joined in the Sisters' celebrations by hoisting the flag on an eighteen-foot pole. While the symbols flying above the partially-finished convent may not have represented every nationality of the community, there is no doubt that the Sister Provincial was well spoken for by the rose thistle. The celebrations were fittingly concluded with a large cake which the Sisters of Mercy sent out to the Sisters via the ever-faithful messenger, Father McAuliffe.[25]

Although Father Woods had been expected in Bathurst within a few weeks of the Sisters' arrival, he did not reach there until 25 September 1872. The following day he travelled out to The Vale where he celebrated Mass for the Sisters. Teresa thought she had 'never [seen] FD [Father Director] so happy nor look so well.'[26] That same day he and Bishop Quinn travelled to Maitland where Woods spent the following three weeks giving missions and directing retreats.

The Sisters were undoubtedly delighted to welcome Father Woods to The Vale and valued the instruction he would provide throughout the following year. But though they continued to refer to him as 'Father Director', the Diary and Teresa's letters portray a certain sense of reserve where he is concerned. The troubles of

---

23. Quinlan to Walsh, 23.7.1872.
24. Diary, 15.8.1872.
25. Diary, 7.9.1872.
26. McDonald to MacKillop, 29.9.1872. Diary, 26.9.1872.

Adelaide were still fresh in their minds. They were all aware that the Commission of Inquiry had recommended that Woods be relieved of all responsibility for the Sisters of St Joseph and the Institute—even if that recommendation would not be confirmed by Rome for some months.[27] They were also aware that Bishop Quinn, to whom they now owed respect and obedience, was one of the very bishops who had made that initial recommendation. Also fresh in their minds was the power—and sometimes misuse of power—exerted by bishops. There can be no doubt therefore, that they would have carefully avoided any situation or action which might have antagonised Bishop Quinn.

It was Teresa, however, who was most cautious regarding Woods' position with the community. Not only did she share all the reservations of her Sisters but her personal experience of Woods when she was Provincial in Adelaide made her especially vigilant. During those troubled times she had come to see the Father Director in a different light. The trust she once had in his direction and guidance had waned. Not long after she met with Woods at The Vale, Teresa described her feelings to Mary: '. . . you know I am much weaned from him now and I am not so much afraid as I used to be.'[28] Indeed, her trust in God, her commitment to the Institute, and her wisdom, courage and common sense had been refined in the adversity of Adelaide. Increased self-confidence made her unafraid of putting forward her opinion. So it was that when Woods told Teresa that Mary Joseph had asked to join the Institute, Teresa did not give him an answer. Rather, as he had requested, she passed on the message to Mary, but she also consulted Father McAuliffe.[29] She expected that, as Mary Joseph's confessor, he could be relied on to give sound advice. There could well have been another reason for Teresa's hesitancy. Woods had previously shown a remarkable lack of judgement regarding Mary Joseph.[30] The

---

27. The judgement that Woods was 'not capable of directing a religious family' and the directive that 'he is to be removed from the leadership and direction of the Sisters of St Joseph and that . . . another upright and suitable priest is to be nominated,' was issued by Propaganda Fide on 25 May 1873. Archives of Propaganda Fide, Rome: SOCG 1873 vol. 1000, folios 1239 – 1246v. <www.library.unisa.edu.au/condon/CatholicLetters/> Accessed 9 April 2016.
28. McDonald to MacKillop, 29.9.1872.
29. McDonald to MacKillop, 29.9.1872.
30. MacKillop to Woods, 5.3.1870; Woods to MacKillop, 20.6.1870; MacKillop to Woods, 8.7.1870. McKenna, With Grateful Hearts, 109–110.

Provincial could well have doubted his present capacity to assess prudently the young woman's suitability for religious life.

Whatever of that, Bishop Quinn judged Mary Joseph to be an acceptable candidate for the Institute with the proviso that her vows be taken on a yearly basis.[31] On the feast of All Saints he made a special trip to The Vale to receive her as a postulant in the presence of all the people who had gathered for Mass. She took the name Sister Aloysius of Our Lady of Dolours.[32] While always retaining a childlike character she was to prove a faithful Sister of St Joseph until events at The Vale three years later would change the course of her life.

Some five weeks after the Sisters had raised the celebratory flag to signify the conclusion of the brickwork of the new convent, the building was finally completed. There was great excitement among the Sisters as they prepared for the move into their new home. While the living conditions during the months since their arrival had been difficult, and they had felt their isolation from the Mother House, the four women had done remarkably well. The Josephite tradition had been firmly established, numbers in the school had doubled and the village people had come to know and respect the veiled women who so obviously cared for their welfare.[33] Teresa could well be pleased with the first Josephite foundation in New South Wales. She was also delighted to be able to give a good report of her health to the Sister Guardian. 'You will be surprised dear Sister,' she wrote to Mary, 'when you hear that I am so well. This place seems to agree with me so well.'[34]

---

31. According to the 1868 Rule, a woman who wished to join the Institute worked in the school with the Sisters for a couple of months. She then was received as a postulant—a period which spanned at least three months. She then was invested or clothed with the habit (formally 'received') into the Institute. After at least one year she made vows for one year. At the conclusion of that year, she made vows for two years. At the conclusion of that period, she made vows for life. Each of these steps was taken only at the desire of the Sister and with the approval of the Sisters. The four vows were poverty, chastity, obedience and to promote the love of Jesus, Mary and Joseph in the hearts of little children. Supposition suggests that in Mary Joseph's case, due to her past mental instability, Bishop Quinn allowed her entry to the Institute on the understanding that she would make her vows each year rather than for life.

32. McDonald to MacKillop, 4.11.1872. Diary, 1.11.1872.

33. For the increasing numbers of the school roll see McDonald to MacKillop, 14.9.1872; Dwyer to MacKillop, 29.9.1872; Braham to MacKillop, 23.11.1872.

34. McDonald to MacKillop, 14.9.1872.

As they prepared for the opening of their new convent, the Sisters of St Joseph were on the cusp of development and expansion throughout the Bathurst diocese.

Teresa of the Incarnation

13
At The Vale

It was mid-October 1872 when the bricklayers and carpenters finally packed their tools and farewelled the Sisters. The painting was to be left until later when the Sisters would do it themselves in order to save the diocese that expense.[1] Such was their relief at finally having their own living space that they decided to occupy the rooms immediately, although the official opening would not take place until Sunday 10 November.

Prior to the move, the entire building required cleaning. Father McAuliffe, who arrived to assist, appointed himself as the supervisor of those scrubbing the floors. Not satisfied with their first attempt, he directed the 'big girls' who had been assigned to the task to 'scrub every room twice to make the boards look white.'[2] Their work finally completed to his satisfaction and the warmth of the October day having dried the spotless floors, the Sisters spent their first night in the dormitory of the convent on 16 October 1872.[3]

After a night of heavy rain, dark clouds still hung over The Vale on the morning of 10 November. Fortunately the skies cleared as from 9.00 am a cavalcade of buggies, horsemen, people on foot, and the school children dressed in white and carrying appropriate banners gathered to escort the official party through the village and to the convent. After the opening and blessing by Bishop Quinn, Father McAuliffe celebrated Mass. The sermon, which lasted for over an hour

1. McDonald to MacKillop, 4.11.1872. For some unknown reason the Sisters did not do the painting. Late in January 1873 professional painters were employed for the task. Diary, 24.1.1873.
2. Diary, 16.10.1872.
3. McDonald to MacKillop, 21.10. 1872.

and was preached by Father Dillon, praised the Sisters whose 'vow is poverty, their object education and compassion for the poor, the sick and the afflicted.'[4] The 500 people present responded generously to his words by clearing the debt on the building and leaving a balance of £30.00 for further use. In the afternoon, the people enjoyed refreshments in a marquee erected in the grounds, while Teresa and the Sisters provided lunch for the bishop and clergy in the reception room.[5]

The community was delighted with the convent—'a neat little conventual-looking building, consisting of a reception room, community room, dormitory and kitchen.'[6] Because no provision had been made in the convent for an oratory, the Sisters continued to use the church for that purpose. Within days of the opening they were visited by two Sisters of Mercy from Bathurst and two Sisters of Charity who were visiting the town. The Diary records how delighted Teresa and the community were to welcome 'real nuns'—indicating that the Josephites were conscious of their newness to religious life both individually and as a recently-founded Australian Institute.[7]

Because there was no room to accommodate postulants in the cramped conditions of the church, the first three women who applied to join the Institute at The Vale travelled to Adelaide where they were received as postulants.[8] Teresa and the Sisters had met and accepted them as candidates prior to their journey to Adelaide—as had Father Woods and Bishop Quinn. However, not all those who wished to join the Institute were accepted. When a young woman who had been accepted by the bishop and Woods during their time at Maitland presented herself at The Vale, the Sisters judged her unsuitable for the religious life and in particular for the demanding conditions often required of the Josephite lifestyle. Though Bishop Quinn, and in particular Woods, pressed Teresa to accept the candidate, she

---

4. *Freeman's Journal*, 16.11.1872, 52. Father Dillon was the parish priest of Camden and a friend of Father Woods.
5. McDonald to MacKillop 20.11.1872. Diary, 10.11.1872.
6. Tobin, *History*, 1.
7. Diary, 15.11.1872; McDonald to MacKillop, 20.11.1872.
8. Sisters Marcella Dwyer of Bathurst, Editha Flanagan of Sydney and Liguori McGrath of Sydney. Sister Aloysius Braham—Mary Joseph who had accompanied the Sisters to The Vale—had already been received as a postulant. McDonald to MacKillop, 21.8.1872; 14.9.1872; 17.9.1872; 21.9.1872; 29.9.1872.

remained firm. Only later did both men acknowledge the forthright manner and wisdom of the Provincial.[9]

The first young women after Sister Aloysius Braham to join the Sisters of St Joseph at The Vale arrived within weeks of the opening of the convent. The English-born Elizabeth Welsh (Sister Matthew) had been living in Maitland. Matilda O'Gorman (Sister Gertrude) had been living in Sydney since her arrival from Ireland.[10] The three postulants—Sisters Aloysius, Matthew and Gertrude—soon settled into a programme of instruction arranged by Teresa who now took on the added responsibility of mistress of postulants. Twice a day they met for instruction in the religious life, and in the Josephite spirit and Rule and teaching method. The Vale novitiate had begun.[11] A fourth postulant would arrive on Christmas Eve—Catherine Kevearney who took the name Sister Patrick.

While the initial increase in numbers gave a great boost to the community, Teresa could not help feeling apprehensive about what Bishop Quinn might be planning for the Sisters. As early as August he had told Teresa he wanted to discuss some aspects of the Rule with Mary MacKillop. At the same time Father McAuliffe had warned Teresa not to give the bishop any impression that there were Sisters at The Vale who might be spared to establish another foundation. She had seen some of the results of sending out on mission Sisters who were untrained in the religious life and in teaching method and practice. She did not want those outcomes repeated in the Bathurst diocese. Late in the year she wrote of her concerns to Mary:

> The bishop seems most anxious to scatter the Sisters and I am not at all inclined for such a thing. I would rather let the two professed [Sisters] go than send the postulants until after their profession. They are not fit to be sent anywhere yet. I think, dear Sister that you think the same, that is to keep the novices and postulants in the novitiate until they are professed.[12]

But as the year drew to a close, there was no indication that Teresa's fears might be realised. The community was taken up in preparation

9. McDonald to MacKillop, 14.10.1872; 9.11.1872. Diary, 2.12.1872.
10. McDonald to MacKillop, 20.11.1872.
11. McDonald to MacKillop, 26.11.1872.
12. McDonald to MacKillop, 26.12.1872.

for the school examinations and distribution of prizes to be held on Friday 20 December. It was an important day for the Sisters whose teaching proficiency, and indeed worth in the diocese, would be judged on the results.

Bishop Quinn, six priests (one of whom was Father Woods) and a number of parents were greeted by enthusiastic students and a schoolroom displaying all manner of ornamental and practical work. The oral examinations covering all subjects were successfully completed and prizes were distributed, interspersed with songs and recitations by the students. During the bishop's address he thanked the Sisters and parents for 'a highly efficient school of over 50 children.' He gave a special vote of thanks to Father McAuliffe 'to whose zeal and assiduity the convent and church owed its existence.' He then celebrated the beginning of the school holidays by distributing sweets and fruit among the students.[13] It had been a successful day for everyone concerned.

Father Woods had returned to Bathurst four days prior to the opening of the convent. From that time until the end of the year he was busy with retreats for the clergy and the boarders at the Sisters of Mercy School, and with the giving of missions and the Forty Hours devotion in various Mass centres around Bathurst.[14] He also paid frequent visits to The Vale convent celebrating Mass, giving instructions to the Sisters or joining them for recreation. Late in December he gave the community a six-day retreat at the conclusion of which Sister Hyacinth made her life vows.[15] Teresa later described the retreat as 'a most wonderful one to all of us. I never spent such a happy one and all the Sisters say the same. It was the most practical one

---

13. *Freeman's Journal*, 4.1.1873, 4. Among the prize winners were Elizabeth Kent and Elizabeth Punyer who both joined the Institute a few years later taking the names Sister Clare and Sister Stanislaus respectively.

14. Diary, 13.11.72 – 9.12.72. MacKillop, *Julian Tenison Woods*, 193–195. Anne Player rsj, *Julian Tenison Woods 1832–1889: The Interaction of Science and Religion*. Thesis submitted for the degree of Master of Arts. Australian National University, 1990, Appendix A. The Forty Hours devotion was a period of some forty hours during which the Blessed Sacrament was exposed in a monstrance on the altar of the church and people gathered for special prayers. It concluded with Benediction—a short liturgical ceremony during which the priest blessed the congregation with the raised Blessed Sacrament and special hymns were sung.

15. Perthville *Register*, 27.12.1872.

I ever heard.'[16] Sister de Sales Tobin, writing 10 years later and from accounts given her by the Sisters who attended the retreat, recorded that they loved to speak of the practical instructions Father Woods gave. It was a retreat 'the recollection of which they ever cherished.'[17] After celebrating Christmas at Bathurst, Woods farewelled the Sisters and prepared to leave for Queensland. From there he would move to Tasmania. It would be February 1877 before he would return to The Vale. That retreat of December 1872—so valued and enjoyed by Teresa—was destined to be her last meeting with Father Woods.

As Teresa and her Sisters looked back on 1872, they could be well pleased. They had made the transition from Adelaide, successfully established the Institute in the Bathurst diocese, demonstrated their teaching expertise and attracted new members to their ranks. On a local level they had become known as women who cared for the children they taught, who were interested in the wellbeing of the villagers and who sought out and visited the sick and the troubled of any or no religious belief. Bishop Quinn readily acknowledged the success of the foundation: '. . . the Sisters are getting on very well indeed in every way.'[18] The new year of 1873 would usher in a change of focus. The former emphasis on establishment would change to that of expansion as more young women joined the Institute, and convents and schools opened in new centres. For Teresa too, the New Year brought changes both personally and in her role as Provincial.

While she had kept well during the first months at The Vale, Teresa became ill late in November 1872. Such was the pain she endured 'round the heart' for some fifteen minutes, that she thought she would die. At that time too she endured the return of the headaches which had troubled her in the past. Her only relief was to rest in bed.[19] Father McAuliffe, who worried that the Sisters did not have enough to eat, ordered Teresa to 'eat meat, drink wine and sleep until 7o'c for a week.'[20] But the relief she gained from following his instructions was only temporary. By the end of February she was confined again to her

---

16. McDonald to MacKillop, 26.12.72.
17. Tobin, *History*, 2.
18. Quinn to MacKillop, 14.1.1873.
19. McDonald to MacKillop, 26.11.1872.
20. McDonald to MacKillop, 26.11.1872.

bed with severe headaches which affected her vision.[21] Sisters Joseph
and Aloysius did all they could to assist Teresa whose workload as
mistress of postulants had increased. Sometime in January Anne
Tobin, who had run the denominational school at The Vale prior to
the Sisters' arrival, joined the Institute taking the name Sister de Sales.
A well-educated woman, she was able to assist Teresa in the teaching
of the postulants thus providing some relief for the Little Sister.[22]

There were also some difficulties emerging among the Sisters.
Although Teresa had been relatively few years in religious life,
experience had taught her that 'in young communities there are many
things to fear and be anxious about.'[23] Sister Hyacinth Quinlan, whose
inclination towards depression had emerged during the troubles of
Adelaide, became 'quite dejected' and, as Teresa recognised, 'in her
spiritual troubles.'[24] Sometimes sulking, sometimes angry, sometimes
in tears and on occasions refusing to leave her bed, she disturbed
the entire community. Teresa, who took the responsibility of Little
Sister and Provincial very seriously, used a gentle approach towards
Hyacinth with mixed results.

But there was also good news with the arrival of three Sisters
from Adelaide. Bishop Quinn had long pressed Mary MacKillop for a
community of Josephites for Bourke. Although the Sisters allocated to
that foundation could have made their way from Adelaide to Bourke
via the Murray and Darling rivers, the low water level had prevented
their sailing. Instead they came to The Vale from where it was thought
they would travel to Bourke.[25] The joy of welcoming their own Sisters
is evident in the Diary entry for 1 February: 'To our great delight the
carriage drove up about half past seven and we once more saw three
of our very own Sisters from dear old Adelaide.'[26] They had arrived
just in time for Aloysius' reception as a novice which was conducted

---

21. McDonald to MacKillop, 27.2.1873.
22. McDonald to MacKillop, 14.1.1873.
23. McDonald to MacKillop, 14.1.1872.
24. McDonald to MacKillop, 14.1.1872. McDonald to MacKillop, 22.3.1873.
    MacKillop to Woods, 16.9.1871, 26.9.1871.
25. Quinn to MacKillop, 14.1.1873.
26. Diary, 1.2.1873. Sister Joseph Mary Fitzgerald—later known as Josephine
    probably to avoid confusion with Sister Joseph Dwyer—was professed, as was
    Sister Philomena. Sister Helena Myles, one of the former 'visionaries' of Adelaide,
    was a novice.

by Bishop Quinn the following morning. It was the first reception of a novice at The Vale.[27]

It was not until the Sisters had arrived from Adelaide that Bishop Quinn realised he could not afford their fares from Bathurst to Bourke. Teresa, unsure of what plans he had for the new arrivals, worried that he would arrange another foundation for which she would be required to supply Sisters. So far she had stood firm against appointing postulants or novices to teaching positions until after their profession. But Quinn was anxious to open as many schools as possible as quickly as possible, and he expected Teresa to supply the necessary teachers.

So when he told her of his decision to open a convent and school at Wattle Flat, Teresa knew that she had no option but to appoint a community.[28] She pondered the possibilities. Sisters Joseph Mary (Josephine) Fitzgerald and Philomena Galvin were both professed and had been sent from Adelaide with the Bourke appointment in mind. But Teresa was fearful of sending Sister Helena Myles away from The Vale. She felt the novice, one of the former Adelaide 'visionaries', would benefit from further training and having Father McAuliffe as her confessor. In the end she chose Sister Matthew Welsh, who had been a postulant since November 1872. The Provincial also decided to accompany the community to Wattle Flat and see them established.

Teresa encountered difficulties even before she set out with the Sisters. When the parish priest, Father D'Arcy, called at The Vale convent he asked Teresa to postpone their arrival at Wattle Flat for a short time so that he could ensure that all was in readiness to receive the community. Teresa, who considered him 'a great gentleman [who] likes things good and nice', was unsettled by this request. She wrote to Mary MacKillop:

> I took the opportunity of speaking to him about what we usually had in our houses, also that we were accustomed to make our foundations ourselves and were prepared to meet many difficulties. I am afraid he intends coming with us and I

27. Diary, 2.2.1873.
28. Situated thirty-five kilometres north of Bathurst, the town of Wattle Flat had been a thriving gold mining town of some 2,000 people during the 1850s. By the time of the Josephite foundation, that number had dwindled to just a few hundred.

do not like clergymen going about with nuns. Even the Bishop said if he had been home he would come with us. May our dear Lord deliver us from such company. I am very fond of priests but I like them in their place.[29]

The experienced Provincial might have had to accede to the bishop's wishes regarding the new foundation, but she was not going to be dictated to by anyone who might interfere with the simplicity and poverty integral to the Josephite spirit. Then, almost as though surprised by her forthright words, she added: 'However I am sure our dear Lord will dispose of all for the best, welcome be His holy will.'

As it was, Teresa and the Sisters did not arrive in Wattle Flat until Sunday 9 March. It was a long journey over a rough road. After leaving The Vale in the bishop's carriage and four greys and stopping for the 8.00 am Mass in Bathurst, they finally arrived at their destination about 2.00 pm. They were met by a crowd of grateful people—mostly gold diggers who had fallen on hard times after the reefs had been worked out. Teresa was reassured that the Josephite poverty would not be encroached upon when she saw the convent—'two small shells of rooms . . . worse than what we had at The Vale'—that had been added to the rear of the church.[30] Because they had no facilities for cooking for the first two days, Father D'Arcy arranged for their meals to be supplied from one of the public houses. Four days after their arrival, they opened school in the 'very shaky looking building' which also served as a church. Of the 34 pupils who arrived on the first day, the older ones were surprisingly advanced but their teachers found the younger children had been much neglected.[31]

Teresa stayed for two weeks helping the community to set up the convent and school. Unfortunately, she caught a severe cold and was laid up for the final three days. She was also deeply distressed by a quarrel between Josephine and Philomena. The serious admonition she gave them reduced Josephine to recognition of her responsibility and a sincere apology, whereas Philomena informed the Provincial that she would remain at Wattle Flat only until she could be replaced.[32]

29. McDonald to MacKillop, 27.2.1873.
30. McDonald to MacKillop, 13.3.1873.
31. McDonald to MacKillop, 13.3.1873.
32. McDonald to MacKillop, 26.3.1873. Philomena had caused disruption in The Vale community almost since the day of her arrival there. When Teresa realised

On her return to The Vale, Teresa asked Father McAuliffe if he would offer Philomena some advice regarding what seemed to be her antipathy for Josephine. While he did not wish to encroach on the territory of another priest, he promised to do what he could.[33] Since their arrival in the diocese, McAuliffe had proved himself to be a prudent and true friend to the Sisters. A product of both the times and the Church, his proprietorial and paternalist relationship with the community grates upon modern ears. Yet his care for all the Sisters was sincere and generous and they held him in deep affection. Teresa found him a wise sounding- board—not only in dealing with Philomena but also in assisting Hyacinth.[34] Whether Teresa had consulted with Father Woods during his time at Bathurst the previous year seems unlikely given the decisions of the Commission of Inquiry and her distrust of his direction. But from early in 1873 she had further reason not to seek his advice. Bishop Quinn forbade Teresa or the Sisters to seek spiritual advice from Father Woods or to have any private communication with him.[35] Teresa was not perturbed by this prohibition. 'I can assure you we have no better friend anywhere than Father McAuliffe,' she wrote to Mary. 'He more than supplies FD's place here with us. Still dear Sister we never forget FD.'[36]

When Teresa settled back into The Vale community after her time in Wattle Flat, she began to prepare four of the postulants for their reception of the habit which was to take place in April. Prior to the

---

the new arrival had very poor eyesight, she had her eyes tested and glasses prescribed in the hope that this might make Philomena feel better about herself. McDonald to MacKillop, 27.2.1873.

33. McDonald to MacKillop, 26.3.1873.

34. McDonald to MacKillop, 4.2.1873.

35. McDonald to MacKillop, 4.2.1873. Bishop Quinn's desire to have Woods give missions, retreats and other devotions throughout the diocese seems to have overridden his wish to prevent him from giving any spiritual direction to the Sisters—as the Commission of Inquiry had recommended. Therefore, in order that Woods' work in the diocese from October to Christmas 1872 run smoothly and productively, Quinn did not prevent him from visiting the Sisters at The Vale. However, once that work had been completed and Woods had left the diocese, the bishop issued the Sisters with the prohibition against communication with him. While records do not indicate that Quinn gave the same prohibition to Woods, Teresa's letters to Mary confirm that Woods continued to write to the Sisters at The Vale.

36. McDonald to MacKillop, 26.3.1873.

ceremony she conducted a retreat of three days for those who were to be received. On 14 April Bishop Quinn formally received Sisters Matthew Welsh, Gertrude O'Gorman, de Sales Tobin and Patrick Kevearney. Later in the year the first profession ceremony took place at The Vale when Sister Helena Myles made her vows on 17 August 1873.[37] Numbers continued to increase as 1873 progressed. By July Teresa reported to Mary that there were 11 Sisters at The Vale—two professed, six novices and three postulants—'all well and exceedingly happy thank God.' Counting the three Sisters at Wattle Flat, the number of Sisters of St Joseph in the diocese had increased to 14.[38]

Late in March, The Vale community received a circular from Mary MacKillop informing the Sisters that she was about to leave for Rome, 'to the feet of the Holy father, there to implore his sanction for our holy Rule.'[39] Since the conclusion of the Commission of Inquiry in June 1872, moves had begun to ensure some standing and security for the Institute. Father Woods and both Father Reynolds and Tappeiner suspected that the bishops in whose diocese the Sisters worked would exert influence in Rome to change some aspects of the Josephite Rule – most significantly the principle of central government.[40] They therefore felt it imperative that the Rule be personally presented in Rome by Mary in order that its integrity would be preserved and that it would conform to the requirements of the Roman authorities. She left Adelaide on 28 March 1873.

Meanwhile, the Sisters at The Vale and Wattle Flat carried on. Both schools were doing well. The problems in the Wattle Flat community were solved after Teresa moved Philomena back to The Vale to be under her watchful eye. Hyacinth, who had recovered from her bout of depression and spiritual troubles, was appointed Little Sister at 'The Flat'—as it was affectionately called by the Sisters. A new convent,

---

37. Perthville *Register*. Tobin, *History*, 2.
38. McDonald to MacKillop, 6.7.1873. Records confirm that numbers at The Vale increased as more women joined the Institute. Early documentation was not well kept and some names can be picked up only in the Diary and in letters with no indication as to whether these women remained in the Institute or chose to leave. Consequently it is impossible to know the particulars of some women or the details of their time in the Institute.
39. MacKillop to the Sisters, Feast of the Annunciation, 1873 in *Mother Mary's Circulars to the Sisters* (Sydney: Sisters of St Joseph, 1976), 3.
40. Woods to MacKillop, January, 1873; MacKillop to the Sisters, 23.3.1873.

completed late in 1873, meant that living conditions for the Sisters vastly improved. Teresa, whose health continued to deteriorate, carried on as Provincial, Little Sister at The Vale and Mistress of postulants and novices.[41] As the Sisters prayed for the success of Mary's request in Rome and her safe return, they were unaware that the Institute in the Bathurst diocese was on the threshold of a major upheaval.

---

41. In July 1873 Joseph Dwyer wrote to Mary MacKillop that Teresa 'has not been well for the last few months.'

14
The Clouds Gather

Soon after New Year 1874, the Sisters and students returned to school. Life at The Vale and Wattle Flat took on the familiar timetable of classes and the many other works of charity and devotion to which the Sisters gave their time.[1]

Although after her departure for Rome Mary MacKillop was unable to keep up a regular correspondence with Teresa, the Bathurst Provincial received weekly letters from Adelaide. Father Tappeiner, in his role of Spiritual Director of the Institute, also wrote to Teresa. She had expected that Father Woods might call sometime around Christmas 1873 on his way to Tasmania, but that was not to be.[2] His three years in Tasmania, however, were to prove fruitful for The Vale community in an unexpected way. From the time of his arrival

---

1. During Mary MacKillop's time overseas (28.3.1873–4.1.1875), little correspondence to and from The Vale is extant. The Diary dates from: 22.7.1872–2.2.1873 and from 29.10.1874–22.4.1875. The Trunkey Creek Diary dates from 10.1.1875– 22.3.1875. It is evident that from early in 1873, there are gaps in the Diary. With these resources missing, information about that period is limited.
2. McDonald to MacKillop, 6.7.1873. Press discusses two reasons for Woods' decision to move directly from Queensland to Tasmania stopping briefly in Melbourne. He wanted to get away from the complications of dealing with the Bishops Matthew and James Quinn (of Bathurst and Brisbane respectively) and their cousin, Bishop Murray of Maitland. More significantly, such was the hurt he felt when Mary went to Rome without meeting and consulting with him, that he sought the friendly face of Bishop Murphy of Tasmania and a diocese removed from the mainland where he could continue his missionary work. In fact Mary had tried to contact Woods, but because he was on missionary work in outback Queensland her letters failed to reach him before her departure. Woods to Phillips, 21.4.1873. Press, *Julian Tenison Woods*, 152–159. McKenna, *With Grateful Hearts*, 134–135.

there during the last week of February 1874, Woods' missionary work inspired a number of women to seek entry into the religious communities with which he was associated. At least four of the thirteen entrants at The Vale in 1874 were from Tasmania.[3]

It was in June 1874 that Bishop Quinn set out on his *ad limina* visit to Rome.[4] Apart from fulfilling the obligation of all bishops in Australia at that time to visit Rome every 10 years, he was hoping to recruit priests and religious for the diocese. He was also planning to influence the Roman authorities regarding the Rule of the Sisters of St Joseph. In particular he wished to change the fundamental tenet of central government by the Sister Guardian, to government by the bishop of each diocese in which the Sisters worked. He also wished to change that section of the Rule which prohibited the teaching of instrumental music. Behind his thinking was a conviction that the Sisters of St Joseph would be a successful work force in a diocese provided they could not be withdrawn, or in any way changed, by an authority beyond the bishop's complete control. He was also convinced that Catholic schools would be more appealing to parents if lessons in instrumental music were available. Another reason Quinn thought the teaching of music to be advantageous was that it would provide an income for the Sisters.[5] Quinn's mind on these matters was made prior to The Vale foundation. He hoped that after the Sisters were settled into the diocese and dependent on him, they would comply with his orders without question. However, Mary MacKillop's impending request in Rome to have the Rule approved roused him to action. In a letter to Monsignor Kirby written soon after Mary's departure, he asked his agent in Rome to assist Mary by all means. But he also requested Kirby 'to impress' upon the Cardinal

---

3. Perthville Register. Diary, 22.11.1874. McDonald to MacKillop, 24.1.1875. Teresa states that eight women 'were sent by Father Julian,' but it is impossible to verify that number.

4. *Ad limina—* to the threshold or door of the Apostles.

5. Quinn to Kirby, 18.4.1873. From 1849 Monsignor Tobias Kirby was Rector of the Irish College in Rome and the agent in Rome of the Irish bishops of Australia. The prohibition against the teaching of music was based on Woods and MacKillop's view that music was a luxury enjoyed by the wealthy and that if undertaken it might cause essential educational needs to suffer, distinction among the Sisters that might result in disturbance in the community and more attention being paid to those who had the resources to pay.

Prefect of Propaganda Fide, Cardinal Barnabo, his own observations and wishes.[6] When he reached Rome the following year, he would make his own more direct representations.

Bishop Quinn, however, left his run too late. On the last day of June 1873, Mary wrote to her trusted advisors in Adelaide that the opinion of authorities in Rome was that central government in the Rule must be strengthened and this included the approval of only one novitiate for the training of the young Sisters. She was disappointed that the very strict poverty of the Institute was rejected by the authorities, but accepted that the Institute should possess land, money and income in its own right.[7] While agreeing that music did not belong in schools conducted by the Sisters, the authorities made no formal reference to what they considered to be the teaching of a subject, and therefore was a matter for the Sisters. The revised Rule or 'Constitutions' gave the Superior General of the Institute full domestic authority over its government and administration. It also specified the rights of the bishop in his own diocese. He was responsible to appoint confessors for the Sisters, to examine postulants and novices regarding their suitability for religious life and to discipline grave faults among the Sisters. The Constitutions also specified that he was not permitted to interfere with the appointment of Sisters to various houses and works, with the Superior General's visitation of the convents in every diocese or with the holding of Chapters. In addition, he was not permitted to change the Constitutions. Henceforth the Institute was to be placed under the care of a Cardinal Protector in Rome. Cardinal Franchi, the Institute's first Protector, proved a strong and wise support to Mary MacKillop.[8]

Although at that time the Constitutions had not been given the status of a formal decree, they carried the weight of Roman authority. Mary, aware of Bishop Quinn's plans for the Institute, did not want to give him the opportunity of interfering in this tacit approval. She knew too that in his desire to get news of her request to Rome, he would question the Bathurst Provincial, Teresa. Therefore, in order to

---

6. Quinn to Kirby, 18.4.1873.
7. MacKillop to Sisters Calasanctius Howley, Monica Phillips and Francis Xavier Amsinck, 30.6.1873 in *Mother Mary's Circulars to the Sisters*, 17–22.
8. Foale, *The Josephite Story*, 130–131.

protect Teresa from possible awkward situations, Mary directed that she not be told at that time of the developments in Rome.[9]

Bishop Quinn seems not to have become aware of the decisions made by Rome until he arrived there sometime in August 1874. He was extremely annoyed that 'a woman who had never spent one hour in religious training' had such influence with Propaganda while his representations were overlooked.[10] From that time onward in Rome and more strongly after he returned to Australia in October 1875, he maintained his conviction that 'the Sisters of St Joseph under the new Constitutions are totally unfit for the circumstances of Australia.'[11]

Meanwhile at The Vale, Teresa made preparations for two new foundations to be made in 1874. The first of these was at German Hill—a locality some 14 kilometres west of Orange. Teresa accompanied the community of three who moved into 'a most uncomfortable building' on a cold winter's day in June.[12] In August Sisters de Sales Tobin, Gertrude O'Gorman and two postulants opened a convent and took over the denominational school at Trunkey Creek, a small town some 50 kilometres south-west of The Vale. Again, Teresa travelled with the Sisters and stayed long enough to see them settled.[13]

School closed that year with the usual examinations which were attended by several priests and a crowd of parents. There was great interest in the display of plain and fancy needlework and the songs and recitations proved very entertaining. After each Sister had successfully examined her own class in all subjects, prizes were distributed. At the end of the day, the Sisters all agreed that 'everything passed off beautifully.'[14]

Although some of The Vale community were very sick with the measles, this did not prevent the Sisters from Wattle Flat, German Hill and Trunkey Creek gathering there for Christmas and a short holiday. The Diary recounts the joy of the Sisters at 'coming home.'[15] Teresa had expected that the extensions to the convent would have

9. MacKillop to Howley, Phillips & Amsinck, 30.6.1873 in *Mother Mary's Circulars to the Sisters*, 21.
10. Quinn to Kirby, 24.9.1874.
11. Quinn to Kirby, 28.1.1876.
12. Tobin, *History*, 4.
13. Tobin, *History*, 3.
14. Diary, 21.12.1874.
15. Diary, 14, 16, 23.12.1874.

provided ample accommodation for the visiting Sisters but, as these were not completed, the Sisters had to make do as best they could.[16] She was disappointed also that a priest could not be found to give the annual retreat. The news that Mary MacKillop had arrived in Adelaide delighted everyone, but especially Teresa. The presence of the Superior General in Australia gave her confidence at a time when her headaches were becoming more severe and Bishop Quinn was threatening to begin his own Institute if decisions about the Rule did not conform to his wishes.[17]

Late in January, Teresa set out again with three Sisters for a new foundation. The locality of Borenore was located twelve kilometres north-west of Orange and about seven kilometres across country from German Hill. The community settled into the convent—a three-room slab construction with inner walls of lath and plaster and a canvas ceiling.[18] Midway through the year the Sisters opened a school at Evans Plains located over the Bald Hill from The Vale. Although a convent was opened there at a later date, in the beginning the Sisters lived in temporary accommodation during the week and returned to The Vale for the weekends.[19] The Evans Plains foundation was destined to be the last that Teresa would make.

Before Teresa set out on the journey to Borenore, she wrote to Mary MacKillop giving an informal report on the Josephite presence in the Bathurst diocese. Three foundations had been established and another was to be made the following week. Numbers had increased remarkably in the previous year, so that on 24 January 1875 the total number of Sisters in the diocese was twenty-eight. While some of the women had been introduced to the Institute through Father Woods in Tasmania, others had come from Sydney and Bathurst, and some from The Vale. Because pressure had been exerted on Teresa to staff schools, she had no option but to appoint the postulants and novices to new foundations. Consequently, six of the novices had spent nearly

---

16. Tobin, *History*, 3. During the second half of 1874 extensions were added to The Vale convent consisting of 'an oratory, large dormitory, refectory, kitchen and other out offices' at a cost of £800.

17. McDonald to MacKillop, undated but after 4.1.1875. Teresa had the information regarding Quinn from a letter written to an unnamed person but likely to be Father McAuliffe.

18. Diary, 28.1.1875. McDonald to MacKillop, 3.2.1875. Tobin, *History*, 4.

19. Dwyer to MacKillop, 18.7.1875.

a year as postulants in the country schools 'partly because they were needed there and partly because it was so difficult to remove them.' Sister Philomena, who after causing a disturbance at Wattle Flat had been moved to The Vale by order of Bishop Quinn, continued to be 'very discontented.' Sister Hyacinth was well and would be appointed Little Sister at Borenore during the next few weeks. Sister Joseph was Little Sister at Trunkey Creek—also well and happy. Sister Aloysius, who was at The Vale, had not been well but she continued to be 'a great help' to Teresa. Her major task was mistress of the boarders. Just days prior to Teresa's letter, and with the completion of the extensions to the convent, the first boarders had arrived at The Vale. Aloysius came into her own with the responsibility for these little children who, according to Teresa's letter, numbered 18. Significantly, Teresa did not mention herself.[20]

The letter portrays the sense that Teresa was pleased with what had been achieved in the two and a half years since they had arrived at The Vale. Leaving aside the difficult Philomena, she told Mary: 'we are all very united.' Teresa wanted Mary to have that assurance in particular about the Bathurst Sisters because, as they both knew, their unity could well be put to the test when Bishop Quinn returned to the diocese later in the year. Teresa's final words to Mary hold an ominous tone—'. . .we are trying to make things tidy now that we have the convent finished . . .' They give a sense of finality and seem to anticipate Joseph's later statement that the Sisters were anxious to pay off their debts 'so that if we have to leave Bathurst we will be able to go without great difficulties in the way of money matters.'[21]

Soon after Mary arrived in Adelaide she convened the First General Chapter of the Institute to be held in Adelaide on 19 March 1875.[22] The purpose of the Chapter was 'to elect Superiors for the next six years' and 'to have laid before it in due form the decisions of the Propaganda with regard to [our] Rule.' The Sisters were also to discuss and make decisions about any 'vexed and tiresome questions' which needed attention. Only those Sisters who had made life vows were eligible to vote, and the Provincials were required to attend in

---

20. McDonald to MacKillop, 24.1.1875; 3.2.1875.
21. Dwyer to MacKillop, 21.6.1875.
22. MacKillop to the Sisters,16.1.1875 in *Mother Mary's Circulars to the Sisters,* 80 – 83.

person. According to the number of Sisters in the Bathurst Province, they were entitled to be represented by one delegate who was also required to attend the Chapter in person. They chose Sister Joseph. Sister Hyacinth was appointed Provincial in Teresa's absence.[23]

The day before Teresa and Joseph left The Vale, Father McAuliffe and other priests from Bathurst and a number of other people called at the convent 'to say farewell for a time to our much and ever-loved Mother Teresa.'[24] These touching words, using the title 'Mother' which was not customary for Provincials, give an indication of the genuine and warm affection in which Teresa was held by the Sisters. She was indeed a loving 'mother' to them and she was 'much and ever-loved' by them.

Beneath these words there is also concern about how Teresa, who continued to be in poor health, would manage the train trip to Sydney and the journey by steamer to Adelaide. Severe headaches were confining her regularly to bed.[25] She also had the added worry of Sister Philomena whose underhand ways caused mischief among the entire community but especially among the newly arrived-postulants. Teresa herself, who treated Philomena with 'such kindness and consideration,' became the butt of her criticism.[26] The Little Sister's words to Mary MacKillop ring with frustration: 'I am obliged to keep her here by order of the Bishop until you would return and then to get her moved . . .'[27] While it seems there may have been some consideration of Philomena travelling to Adelaide with Teresa and Joseph, this was never followed through. Instead she remained at The Vale where Sister Hyacinth the acting Provincial had to cope with her criticism and opposition.

So it was with mixed emotions that Hyacinth and Aloysius waved off their Provincial and Chapter delegate from the Macquarie Plains railway station on 8 March 1875.[28] Thankful that the Institute had at last reached the stage of its first Chapter, they nonetheless worried for Teresa. Yet they were also consoled. Joseph would be a competent

---

23. MacKillop to the Sisters, 16.1.1875. Tobin, *History*, 4. Diary, 6.3.1875.
24. Diary, 7.3.1875.
25. McDonald to MacKillop, 1.2.1875.
26. Quinlan to MacKillop, 14.2.1875.
27. McDonald to MacKillop, 7.2.1875.
28. Diary, 8.3.1875.

and caring travelling companion. And what of Teresa's thoughts as the train puffed its way eastward through the mountains? What of the memories of ships and steamers, of coaches and trains—of the many journeys that had filled her life?

Upon their arrival in Adelaide, Teresa and Joseph were involved immediately in the business of the Chapter. Afterwards there was time for meeting with the Sisters, many of them old friends whom they had not seen since leaving Adelaide three years before. No doubt they also met up with their families and renewed many old acquaintances. Before they left Adelaide the two Sisters wrote a joint letter to Monsignor Kirby thanking him for his assistance to Mother Mary while she was in Rome. Suspecting that Bishop Quinn would seek the aid of the Monsignor in his representations in Rome regarding the Constitutions, they assured Kirby of their loyalty to the bishop. 'We . . . hope that he will be satisfied with the regulations [of the Constitutions] and understand how much our beloved Mother has the interests of his mission at heart and how little she wishes to interfere with his jurisdiction.' Though they acknowledged some difficulties associated with having only one novitiate, they clearly stated that 'we are all firmly convinced of the necessity for it.'[29]

Though there was much during her weeks in Adelaide that Teresa was able to enjoy, it proved to be a difficult time. With ever-deteriorating health, she struggled to keep going and on her return to The Vale looked 'very ill.'[30] She was still far from well when Mary MacKillop visited her Sisters in the Bathurst diocese in August 1875.[31] In order that all the Sisters might have the opportunity to meet with their Superior General, Father McAuliffe closed the schools. By 12 August they had all arrived at The Vale and Mary commenced a retreat during which she explained the Constitutions so recently approved in Rome. At the conclusion of the retreat the professed Sisters renewed their vows according to those Constitutions. This was done with the knowledge and encouragement of Father McAuliffe although it was another Bathurst priest, Father Joseph Horan, who was actually present at the renewal ceremony, rather than Father

29. McDonald and Dwyer to Kirby, 20.4.1875.
30. Tobin, *History* 4.
31. Tobin, *History*, 4. MacKillop to McMullen, 19.1.1876, 3.2.1876. MacKillop to McMullen, 17.8.1875.

McAuliffe. Mary did not allow the postulants or novices to be received into the Institute or make their vows until Bishop Quinn returned to the diocese. Following the retreat, the Sisters returned to the country convents and school resumed.

On her arrival at The Vale, Mary was shocked by Teresa's condition. She wrote of her concerns to Monica Phillips:

> Sister Teresa is far from well; you would not know her. I am really very uneasy about her. She had 11 teeth extracted, her face is puffed up, and all her body so enlarged—something I fear like dropsy. If possible, I must get her to Subiaco or Villa Maria for a change, but this seems next to impossible.[32]

It was with a heavy heart that Mary farewelled her beloved friend.

Teresa of the Incarnate

---

32. MacKillop to Phillips, 17.8.1875.

15

A Priceless Treasure

Early in October, 1875 word reached Bathurst that Bishop Quinn was expected there within weeks. Teresa was having a few days rest at Evans Plains when she got the news.[1] She had recovered to some extent from the swelling of her body but her face was still painful and an ulcer had developed on one of her eyes. There had been some relief from the glasses which had been prescribed, but she was unable to read for any length of time.[2] Thankfully the worry over Sister Philomena had been solved, at least for The Vale community, when she returned to Adelaide with Mary. But with the thought of the bishop's return, Teresa, weakened by illness and concerned for the Institute, was filled with fear. She confided in her trusted friend, Josephine McMullen: 'Will you pray for us as our hour of trial is at hand. I feel so afraid . . . God help us as we are far from home and in a wild country, but God is everywhere or what would become of us?'[3]

Upon his return to the diocese, Bishop Quinn was given an elaborate public reception in Bathurst.[4] The Sisters and pupils at The Vale also welcomed their bishop with special decorations in the school, an address read by one of the children and a selection of songs. Although Teresa had recovered from the worst of the severe illness of August, Bishop Quinn was shocked by her appearance. Speaking to her in private, he limited his criticism of the Constitutions to the provision of a central novitiate, adding that he would write to Mary MacKillop about the matter.[5] It was a happy visit with the Sisters. Sister

---

1. McDonald to MacKillop, 31.8.1875.
2. McDonald to McMullen, 10.10.1875.
3. McDonald to MacKillop, 10.10.1875.
4. *Freeman's Journal,* 30.10.1875. Among the bishop's recruits for the diocese were four young women from County Cork who joined the Sisters of St Joseph.
5. McDonald to MacKillop, 28.10.1875.

Joseph thought that he showed no annoyance over the Constitutions, yet she was cautious. '. . . we are going on as you left us,' she wrote to Mary, 'and we will be faithful to our Mother House and Mother General for ever.'[6]

Before Mary MacKillop left The Vale in August, she had suggested that Teresa should see a doctor who might be able to diagnose the cause of her illness. This suggestion was not followed through until early in November when Teresa had a severe attack of vomiting and palpitations of the heart. After the doctor, who had the reputation of being 'the most experienced medical man in Bathurst' had given his report, Joseph wrote to Mary:

> After sounding S. Teresa, he said that her lungs were quite sound and so was her heart, only that the nerves of the heart were weak and caused that excessive palpitation. The Doctor also said that she had gastric on the stomach which caused the vomiting. However, he assured us that there was nothing serious and that she would be greatly improved in health after this little sickness was over.[7]

Given the medical knowledge and expertise of the time and the respect in which doctors' opinions were held, it is not surprising that the Sisters could 'scarcely contain [their] joy' at the diagnosis. It was 'good news' and they fully expected Teresa to recover. Yet there had been no mention of the severe headaches from which she continued to suffer or of her failing eyesight. Writing some years later of the doctor's visit to Teresa, Sister de Sales remembered that 'he prescribed for her and ordered perfect quiet as she was in so weak a state that excitement or mental exertion of any kind might prove fatal.'[8] She remembered too that his directions were carefully followed. Then, with the advantage of hindsight, she added: '. . . as days and weeks passed, no change for the better had taken place.'

During the weeks following the doctor's first visit to Teresa, she sometimes rallied a little while at other times slipped close to death. By mid-November she was sitting up and beginning to eat a little, although so weak she was unable to a hold a pen.[9] Early on the morning of 22 November, such was her condition that the doctor was

---

6. Dwyer to MacKillop, 27.10.1875.
7. Dwyer to MacKillop, 10.11.1875.
8. Tobin, *History*, 5.
9. Dwyer to MacKillop, 16.11.1875.

called.[10] Either then, or on another occasion, he applied leeches to her stomach. Whatever the hoped outcome of that treatment, it caused 'fits of exhaustion' which the doctor said would pass. By December the palpitations of the heart were 'completely cured,' as was 'the tumour in the stomach.' She would recover from the extreme weakness caused by an attack of 'neuralgic fever,' with continued quiet, rest and care.[11] The noticeable improvement in Teresa's condition about mid-December was attributed partly by the Sisters to her reception of the sacrament of the anointing of the sick. The doctor declared that 'her whole system is in order except the head,' which indicates that she continued to suffer severe headaches. While for some weeks she had needed two Sisters to lift her in and out of bed, she was almost strong enough to do that alone.[12]

During the worst of Teresa's illness, Bishop Quinn had visited her on only a few occasions for a short time. The Sisters were pleased because they did not want her disturbed.[13] Father McAuliffe, however, had called on Sister Joseph. He gave her the news that Bishop Quinn had received a letter from a cardinal stating that Rome had 'no intention of changing the Rule and that he (the Bishop) was to go on as usual in his diocese.' McAuliffe added that this letter— received about a month before—would be forwarded to Mary MacKillop.[14] When she was well enough, Teresa was told of the letter and immediately authorised Joseph to find out if Mary had received such correspondence. The postulants and novices at The Vale would be due for reception and profession by 10 January, and Teresa wanted to be sure the ceremony would be carried out correctly. In fact, Mary had not received such a letter, nor did she ever do so. In view of the approval of the Constitutions by Rome, it is highly unlikely that such a letter could have been written.

In the two months after Bishop Quinn's return to the diocese, he had mentioned the Constitutions only in reference to the central novitiate. Indeed, Joseph had written to Mary that she did not think he would interfere with the Josephites in the diocese.[15] While this could well be explained by the bishop's wish not to disturb Teresa,

10. Braham to MacKillop, 22.11. 1875.
11. Dwyer to MacKillop, 6.12.1875.
12. Dwyer to MacKillop, 6.12.1875; Dwyer to Howley, 13.12.1875.
13. Dwyer to MacKillop, 6.12.1875.
14. Dwyer to MacKillop, 18.12.1875.
15. Dwyer to MacKillop, 16.11.1875.

there could well have been another reason. He later claimed that he was two months back in the diocese before he became aware that Mary had visited The Vale and explained the Constitutions to the Bathurst Josephites, and that all the professed Sisters had renewed their vows according to those Constitutions. On learning that this had happened, he became very angry claiming that Mary had broken an agreement with him.[16] The 'letter' he claimed to have received from the cardinal could well have been a reaction to what he believed to be Mary's breaking of the 'agreement.' Such was his anger that he determined to take immediate action on the whole affair.

Meanwhile, Teresa took a turn for the worse on 18 December— the day before the beginning of the Sisters' retreat at The Vale. Sister Joseph gave an account to Mary MacKillop of what she believed caused the relapse:

> I will tell you, dear Mother, what was the cause of the change on Saturday. Some of the Sisters who were coming home for retreat, after travelling forty miles by the mail coach, had to hire a conveyance in Bathurst to come to The Vale. Well, the manager at the coach office provided them with a grand carriage and pair of greys, so the poor Sisters had to come in it as no other could be had that day. Sister Teresa was up walking round the garden and when she saw the carriage and greys, she concluded that it was the Bishop, and so the blood rushed to her head, and her old sickness returned.

Joseph then tried to reassure Mary:

---

16. Bishop Quinn and Mary MacKillop met in Dublin in September 1874. He later claimed that Mary made an agreement with him that recognised his governance over the Institute in his diocese while allowing that those Sisters who had come from Adelaide should ultimately return there. This agreement was never put in writing and it seems impossible that Mary, whose obedience to Rome and therefore to the Constitutions was faultless, could have made such an agreement. She later explained to him that she had visited the Bathurst diocese at the invitation of Father McAuliffe who had encouraged her in every way to carry out her duties as Superior General while there. However, McAuliffe sought to dissociate himself from the whole affair by asking Mary not to implicate him in any way—which she did not do until a few months later. Quinn to Kirby, 28.1.1876. MacKillop to Quinn, 3.2.1876. Crowley, *Women of The Vale*, chapter 3.

> There is no fear that the Bishop will come while she is so ill, yet she is so fearful. Fr McAuliffe knows the dread the poor Sister has of his Lordship, so his reverence will keep him away as long as possible. We hope that in a few days Sister Teresa will be better.[17]

Teresa did recover enough to sit in the sacristy during some of the lectures given by Father Rice during the retreat. While she had confidence that the Superior General's word was 'the law of every soul in this province,' she evidently did not have that same faith in Father Rice.[18] Taking him aside prior to the first lecture she 'told him not to use his influence in any way over the Sisters in order to make them go with the Bishop against their Mother General and Mother House.' He assured her he would not.[19]

The days of retreat went smoothly and calmly for the thirty-six Sisters, including seventeen postulants, gathered at The Vale. Teresa must have been pleased that she was well enough to welcome them home and participate, to some degree, in the retreat. Not expecting visitors during those days, she was surprised when Bishop Quinn and Father McAuliffe arrived at The Vale on the last afternoon of the retreat—Christmas Eve. But her surprise changed to alarm when the bishop announced that he would speak to all the Sisters—just at that time gathered in the church for a lecture.

In his address he placed before them his objections to the Constitutions. He then told them that he would not allow to remain in the diocese any Sister who chose to follow the Constitutions. It was clear-cut. Those who elected to be under his authority could remain in the diocese. Those who chose to accept the Constitutions under the authority of the Superior General were to leave the diocese. After assuring the Sisters of complete freedom in their choice, he and Father McAuliffe interviewed each professed Sister separately to hear her decision. He did not interview the novices and postulants because he assumed they would remain in the diocese. At the conclusion of the interviews, rather than take any direct action on their outcome, he directed that the Sisters were to return to their convents and open

---

17. Dwyer to MacKillop, 20.12.1875.
18. Dwyer to MacKillop, 18.12.1875.
19. Dwyer to MacKillop, 20.12.1875.

school as soon as possible. This, he said, was to ensure quiet at The Vale for Teresa. He then left The Vale and after celebrating Christmas in Bathurst travelled to Maitland where he stayed for a few days. Father McAuliffe left for a short holiday in Victoria.[20]

So upset was Teresa, so 'grieved,' that her condition worsened to the point that she was 'too weak in mind and body to assist or direct' the Sisters. Whereas prior to Bishop Quinn's ultimatum she had been able to take some small interest in the Sisters and the Institute, now even that was beyond her. Years later Sister de Sales remembered how before the Sisters left The Vale, 'all said a last 'good-bye' to their dear Sister Teresa, who was then sinking fast.'[21].

Left at The Vale were four professed Sisters (besides Teresa), and seventeen postulants. Sister Joseph, who as Assistant Provincial had assisted Teresa during the previous months, was left in that position. The mistress of postulants, Sister Hyacinth, also remained with the postulants. Sister Evangelist Holohan, who had chosen to remain in the diocese under the bishop's authority, was also at The Vale as was Sister Aloysius.[22] At the directive of Bishop Quinn, the six novices had also gone out to the country convents. Joseph had been directed from Adelaide to keep them at The Vale until after their profession— which was due in the New Year. Though she did not refer to the instructions from Adelaide, she did put it to the bishop that they should not be appointed to the country until after their profession. But both Quinn and McAuliffe insisted that they leave at once with the professed Sisters—to ensure peace and quiet for Teresa. Indeed, such was the dilemma in which Joseph found herself, and the difficult situation at The Vale, that she followed their directive. In explaining to Mary MacKillop why she did not obey the Adelaide instruction, Joseph gives an insight into her feelings: 'I was afraid to act according to it for fear of raising war with Fr McA.'[23]

---

20. Dwyer to MacKillop, 3.1.1876, 4.1.1876. MacKillop to Franchi, 11.2.1876. Tobin, *History*, 5.
21. Tobin, *History*, 4–5.
22. Aloysius had initially told Bishop Quinn that she wanted to remain under his authority. She later changed her decision.
23. Dwyer to MacKillop, 4.1.1876. Speculation strongly suggests that Bishop Quinn ordered the novices to leave The Vale because he did not want Teresa influencing their decision regarding the Constitutions.

Events then took an unexpected turn. When the doctor visited Teresa on the 27 or 28 December, he 'ordered' her to the country for a change of air. This seems an extraordinary decision given her deteriorating state. However, the Sisters seemed not to have raised any objection and prepared her to leave for Trunkey Creek which she did on 29 December.[24] One can only imagine Teresa's discomfort as the coach jolted over the fifty kilometres of hilly, rough, country road accompanied by Sister Aloysius and possibly the Sisters appointed to Trunkey Creek. Not only was she leaving the familiarity of The Vale convent—which offered some degree of comfort since the extensions—but she was going to a structure of two rooms and a kitchen.[25] In addition, by going to Trunkey Creek she would be sixty kilometres from the doctor who knew and had been treating her.

The choice of Sister Aloysius to accompany Teresa also raises questions. For some months—and even more so since the deterioration in Teresa's health—Aloysius had been ill. Never of robust health, she succumbed to fainting fits and shaking and sometimes spat blood. But that did not deter her from sitting by Teresa's bed, watching, hoping and even praying that 'Almighty God would give me her illness instead.'[26] Such was the volatile state Aloysius reached at the sight of her 'darling Sister Teresa,' that Joseph 'was afraid she would get insane while Sister Teresa was ill, especially the night she [Teresa] was anointed.'[27] Through the weeks when Teresa had improved a little, Aloysius did regain her health and some stability. But by Christmas, when Teresa's condition became so grave, she became increasingly unstable and unpredictable. Yet it was Aloysius who travelled to Trunkey Creek with Teresa and supposedly would care for her while there.[28]

---

24. Dwyer to MacKillop, 3.1.1876; Dwyer to Howley,19.1.1876.
25. Tobin, *History*, 3–4.
26. Braham to MacKillop, 22.11.1875.
27. Dwyer to MacKillop, 10.11.1875; 6.12.1875.
28. Speculation suggests there may have been another reason for the choice of Aloysius to accompany Teresa. In her dealings with Bishop Quinn about the novices being appointed to the country, Joseph decided not to tell them about the bishop's orders until a final decision had been made. She did this because she knew that the novices had chosen to wait at The Vale for Mary's expected arrival, after which they would be professed according to the Constitutions. She knew too that they would be upset if forced to go to the country. In the meantime, however, Aloysius told the novices the entire situation, causing them to become confused

When Bishop Quinn returned to Bathurst on New Year's Day, he travelled out to The Vale with the intention of sending Teresa to the country for a change of air. But by that time, Teresa had been at Trunkey Creek for three days.[29] During the time there her condition deteriorated rather than improved and it was decided to take her back to The Vale. Once again she was helped into the coach. Once again she endured the jolts and bumps as the horses made their way along the country track. On the morning after her arrival, Monday 10 January, the doctor visited Teresa and gave her 'little hope' of recovery.[30] She was quite conscious during his visit, telling him before he left that she knew she was dying.[31]

For the rest of that day (Monday) and during Tuesday and Wednesday Teresa, though extremely weak, remained conscious and spoke quietly with the Sisters. Bishop Quinn had already removed most of the Sisters from The Vale, giving the reason that he wished Teresa to be left in peace and quiet during her final days. He even gave directions to Joseph that she was not to discuss with Teresa the details of the ultimatum he had given regarding the Constitutions. But neither the bishop nor Father McAuliffe understood the depth of feeling among the Sisters, their warm love for their dying Provincial and their desire to be near her in those last days. Nor did they understand Teresa, who dearly loved her Sisters and who during those days wanted the comfort of their closeness and to know their feelings

and worried about their future and to say 'excitable things.' This put Joseph in a difficult position. The tone of her letter suggests she was annoyed with Aloysius for having caused a great deal of trouble. Suspecting that the future weeks would be ones of uncertainty, confusion and hard decisions, Joseph could well have sent Aloysius to Trunkey Creek to prevent more problems from her indiscretion, loose talk and lack of sound judgement. Dwyer to MacKillop, 4.1.1876. The fact that when Mary MacKillop arrived in Bathurst she immediately sent Aloysius to Adelaide under the care of Sister Gertrude O'Gorman, adds weight to this speculation.

29. Dwyer to MacKillop, 3.1.1876. It seems a coincidence that both the doctor and the bishop suggested a change of air for Teresa. Could it have been that Quinn asked the doctor to order Teresa to the country in order to remove her from The Vale? Her removal would have prevented her from influencing the postulants and Sisters in their choice for or against the Constitution. Could the bishop's visit on New Year's Day have been to check that she had gone to the country, rather than to suggest that she go to the country?

30. Dwyer to Howley, 10.1.1876.

31. Dwyer to Howley, 21.1.1876.

and decisions. During those last precious days, clerical directives faded as the Sisters gathered around Teresa's bed.

Speaking privately with Joseph, Teresa gave every indication of a woman who was in full control of her thinking. 'I am still Sister Provincial, and you are only Sister Assistant; therefore it is your duty to inform me of what is going on in the Convent.'[32] In Joseph's words, they told her 'everything.' Aloysius, who possibly felt guilty about what she had told Bishop Quinn, wanted her 'darling Sister Teresa' to know the truth. She had informed the bishop that she would remain in the diocese under his authority, but that she really intended to adhere to the Constitutions. She also told Teresa that she did that to protect the Provincial and the Mother General from incurring the bishop's blame for influencing the Sisters' decisions. Teresa's reply was simple: '[You] should have told the bishop the truth no matter what the consequences were.'[33] And so the Sisters spoke and prayed with their Provincial and perhaps remembered together when they— Teresa, Joseph, Hyacinth and Aloysius—arrived at the little slab church on that cold winter's day in 1872.

The following day (Tuesday 11 January), Father McAuliffe arrived at The Vale. Teresa continued to remain aware of all that was going on around her. She went to confession, after which she told Father McAuliffe that it was not necessary that she go to the sacrament, but that she 'liked to receive the grace . . . as often as possible.'[34] His visit to Teresa was not, however, the only purpose for his journey to The Vale. He had a message for Sister Joseph from Bishop Quinn. He had decided that Wattle Flat would be the principal house of those who followed the Constitutions. As it had been her decision to adhere to the Constitutions, she was to leave for Wattle Flat immediately.[35] Joseph recounted that 'in about three minutes from this announcement I was on my way to the Flat . . . I was even forbidden to say goodbye to my dying Sister Provincial for fear of disturbing or exciting her.' But Teresa was extremely disturbed by Joseph's absence. So often did

32. Dwyer to MacKillop, 24.1.1876.
33. Dwyer to MacKillop, 24.1.1876.
34. Dwyer to Howley, 21.1.1876.
35. The context of the situation strongly suggests that the major reason for Joseph's removal from The Vale was Bishop Quinn's desire to prevent her from influencing the postulants and other Sisters regarding the Constitutions.

she call out for her, that the Sisters had no option but to explain why Joseph was not there. After hearing how her Sister had been directed to leave The Vale and forbidden to farewell her, Teresa 'mildly and sadly replied, I was placed here by Mother Mary as Sister Provincial, and no person had any authority to send Sister Mary Joseph away without my permission.'[36] Thus, due to that harsh and unfeeling order Teresa, in her final hours, was deprived of the comforting presence of her dear friend. And what of Joseph's feelings as she boarded the 2.00 am coach in Bathurst and travelled through the night to Wattle Flat?

The following day (Thursday 13 January) brought a marked deterioration in Teresa's condition. Father McAuliffe and Bishop Quinn arrived at The Vale about mid-afternoon. The bishop knelt beside her bed praying and speaking kindly to her. During the evening her breathing became weaker. As the prayers for the dying filled the room, Bishop Quinn, 'overcome with grief, sobbed like a child.' Sometime later, he left the room. Joseph Dwyer described Teresa's last moments:

> After he [Bishop Quinn] left the room, Sister Teresa called Father McAuliffe and said, 'Please, Father, give me your blessing.' He did so. She then said, 'Father, put your hand on my forehead and say God's will be done.' He did so and these were her last words to him in this life. The Sisters knelt around her in prayer . . . as [they] were reciting the Litany of St Joseph, just at the last line, 'Zealous for the salvation of souls,' she quietly drew her last breath.[37]

The life of Sister Teresa of the Incarnation, a gentle Scot, a Sister of St Joseph, a 'priceless treasure' had ended at the age of 37 years.[38] It was 10.30 on the evening of Thursday 13 January, 1876. The official cause of her death was given as 'disease of [the] brain.'[39]

Teresa's Solemn Requiem Mass and burial were held on Saturday 15 January 1876 at The Vale. A large number of the village people

---

36. Dwyer to MacKillop, 24.1.1876. Dwyer to Howley, 12.1.1876.
37. Dwyer to Howley, 21.1.1876. As explained in chapter 1, Joseph Dwyer was not present at Teresa's death. This account would have been given to her by those Sisters who were present.
38. MacKillop to Woods, 19.9.1872.
39. Telegram from Quinlan to Howley. Death Certificate of Margaret McDonald.

gathered to farewell a woman who had endeared herself to them by 'her gentleness and kindliness of manner.'[40] The girls who boarded at the convent, dressed in white and wearing black scarves, were also present. The Sisters who knelt in the church and gathered around the grave were filled with sorrow and deep in thought. Confused by the uncertainty of recent weeks and faced with decisions regarding their future, they were caught in a momentous ordeal without the love, support and advice of their beloved Provincial. The Mass was celebrated by Father Cooke, the parish priest of Rockley, and Father McAuliffe preached the sermon. Some thirteen priests attended. Bishop Quinn presided at the ceremonies.[41]

Following the Mass, Teresa was buried so close to the convent that her grave could be seen 'from every door.'[42] Three and a half years before she had decided that rather than stay in the relative comfort of Bathurst, she and the Sisters would move out to the church at The Vale. Her tombstone in the Sisters' Cemetery at Perthville stands as a memorial to her life and to her brief years at The Vale—the spot she called 'our own little place.'[43]

---

40. Tobin, *History*, 2.
41. Records do not indicate whether the Sisters in the country convents attended the funeral. Given the lack of transport at that time and Bishop Quinn's determination to protect the postulants at The Vale from possible influence by those Sisters who had opted for the Constitutions, it is unlikely they did attend. Sister Joseph Dwyer, so harshly ordered away from The Vale prior to Teresa's death, was present at her funeral. Dwyer to Howley, 21.1.1876. *Melbourne Advocate*, 29.1.1876.
42. Dwyer to Calasanctius, 21.1.1876. Later another three Sisters were buried in this cemetery the exact location of which is unknown. At some time about 1886, the remains of the four Sisters were relocated to one grave in the Sisters' present cemetery which is situated behind the Perthville convent. It is marked by a single headstone which bears their names.
43. McDonald to MacKillop, 23.7.1872.

Delivery Form.

[No.

Electric Telegraph, South Australia.

Station, _____ 1876, 12 h 50 m.

		PAID BY SENDER.	UNPAID—TO BE PAID ON DELIVERY.
No. of Words, 6	Telegram	: 2 :	
	Repeating		
Particulars of Charge	Reply		
	Porterage		
Received by	Cab or Boat Hire		

No fee or gratuity to be paid to bearer, unless entered above.

TELEGRAM from _Bathurst_ Station, dated _____ 14 1876.

Addressed to _____

Office Stamp

5	Sister	Provincial	died	half	past
10	ten	O'clock	yesterday	evening	13th Jan
15					
20					

From _Sister Mary Hyacinth_

NOTE.—The Government are not responsible for delays, nor are they responsible for mistakes in the transmission of messages unless the message is repeated, and then to an extent not exceeding £5, vide regulations and conditions.

The telegram sent from Bathurst by Sister Hyacinth Quinlan to Sister Calasanctius Howley in Adelaide informing the Sisters of Sister Teresa McDonald's death.

Sister Teresa McDonald's grave in the Sisters' cemetery at Perthville.

16
Journeys Remembered

Although all the Sisters of St Joseph were acutely aware of their tenuous position in the Bathurst diocese, the uncertainty and anxiety they felt regarding their future gave way to a great sadness during Teresa's last days. They felt deeply the loss of their loved Provincial, but they had little time to mourn her passing. Decisions were to be made. Journeys were to be taken. They awaited the outcome of discussions between Mary MacKillop and Bishop Quinn.

Mary MacKillop's haste to Teresa's bedside had been in vain. She, and three Sisters bound for Brisbane, were in Melbourne when word of Teresa's death reached them on 15 January. Four days later Mary was aboard the steamer *Wentworth* bound for Sydney. From there she wrote to Bishop Quinn: 'I am coming now to see my Sisters in your Diocese.' She left him in no doubt as to the stand she would be taking: 'I cannot do anything against the Constitutions and I trust to your own just disposition, my Lord, not to expect such of me.'[1]

After Teresa's funeral, Joseph Dwyer had asked Quinn for permission to remain at The Vale until the following Tuesday (18 January) when she expected Mary in Bathurst. He refused, adding he 'could not have me [Joseph] spoiling his postulants.' Joseph returned to Wattle Flat unaware that Mary had been delayed in Melbourne and would not reach Bathurst until Saturday 22 January at the earliest.[2]

After Mary's visit to the diocese, she described the events which took place as 'trials' which were 'hard too, though short in Bathurst.'[3] During that week her discussions with the bishop resulted in those

---

1. MacKillop to Quinn, 19.1.1876. The emphasis is Mary's.
2. Dwyer to Howley, 21.1.76. Although the exact date of Mary's arrival in Bathurst is uncertain, records confirm she was there by Sunday 23 January.
3. MacKillop to McMullen, 24.4.1876.

Sisters who remained loyal to the Constitutions gathering their few belongings and preparing to leave for Adelaide. Those who chose to remain in the diocese under the authority of Bishop Quinn assembled at The Vale. This included Sister Hyacinth Quinlan who made a last-minute decision in favour of the bishop. Mary instructed Sister Gertrude O'Gorman to take Aloysius to Adelaide immediately—such was Aloysius' distressed and unpredictable state. Mary herself left the diocese on 31 January. By mid-February 1876, all those 17 Sisters who chose the Constitutions had left the Bathurst diocese. Those at The Vale numbered 14. Though events during that week happened quickly, they took place against and within a complicated web of circumstances and emotions. It was a draining and sad time for all concerned. Within four weeks of Teresa's death, the separation of the Sisters of St Joseph of the Bathurst diocese had taken place.[4]

From the time of their arrival at The Vale, the Josephite community had been overshadowed by uncertainty and insecurity. Each Sister knew of Bishop Quinn's opinion that the Institute was no more than a diocesan group under the authority of the bishop. They had experienced his intrusion into some aspects of their Rule. Though he made few references to his dissatisfaction with the Rule, they suspected that he might take over the complete governance of the Sisters in the Bathurst diocese at any time. Yet each Sister who had renewed her vows according to the Constitutions also knew that she was bound to obey both the Rule and the Sister Guardian under a centralised system of government. That tension—between the authority of the bishop and that of the Sister Guardian—lay at the heart of their insecurity.

Even before their departure from Adelaide, each Sister bound for the Bathurst diocese knew that their Little Sister and Provincial, Sister Teresa, was in poor health. Their letters continually give accounts of her illness and display concern for one whose condition was deteriorating. Integral to their concern for her was their own vulnerability. As their grief over Teresa's approaching death deepened,

---

4. For a full account of the separation of the Bathurst Sisters and for discussion regarding the decisions made by Mary MacKillop, Bishop Quinn and Hyacinth Quinlan see Crowley, *Women of The Vale*, chapter 3. For a complete list of those Sisters who left The Vale for Adelaide in January 1876 and those who remained at The Vale in January 1876 see Crowley, *Women of The Vale*, Appendices III & IV, pages 272–273.

so uncertainty and anxiety increased among the Sisters. These two interwoven situations—grief for Teresa and anxiety regarding their future—ensured a difficult time for all the Josephites in the Bathurst diocese.

The events of the week following Mary MacKillop's arrival in the diocese brought to an end that feeling of insecurity and doubt. Though there was sadness over their consequences, the decisions made by Mary and the bishop enabled the Sisters to gain some security and ease of mind. Finally, they knew where they stood and were able to move on with their lives. And what of Teresa's companions—those who, with her, had made the foundation at The Vale?

As mentioned above, Hyacinth alone stood out from that founding group. She opted to accept the authority of the bishop and to remain at The Vale. There she was appointed by the bishop to the roles of both Sister Guardian and Mistress of novices and postulants. In those positions she played a significant part in Bishop Quinn's establishment of the Diocesan Sisters of St Joseph. Within a few years she had taken a community of Sisters to New Zealand before moving on to Tasmania where she died in 1933. While her life will continue to be overshadowed by controversy, she deserves to be remembered as a Sister of St Joseph who made a rich contribution to the diocesan Josephites. Trained by Mary MacKillop and Father Woods, she threaded their spirit through each community in which she lived—Perthville, New Zealand and Tasmania—and had a formative influence on some members of the foundation communities to Goulburn and Lochinvar.

One of Aloysius's last acts before she left The Vale in January 1876 was to gather together some of her 'darling Sister Teresa's' belongings as keepsakes. Back in Adelaide she became increasingly unsettled. After some weeks she discarded her religious habit and gradually made her way back to Bathurst. Mary MacKillop wrote asking Bishop Quinn to provide her with some care. Father Woods also offered help. Early in 1877 a disturbed and weakened Aloysius returned to The Vale.[5] She died there on 21 March 1877 aged twenty-two years. Her final resting place was next to Teresa in the tiny cemetery beside The Vale Convent.[6] Although Aloysius had been the source of extreme disturbance among the Brisbane Sisters and her inclusion in The Vale

---

5. MacKillop to McMullen, 6.6.1876. MacKillop to Franchi, 12.7.1876. Woods to unknown, 9.3.1877. Mechtilde Woods, 'History', 43.
6. At the time of the establishment of the Sisters' present cemetery at Perthville, Aloysius' remains were relocated there with those of Teresa and two other Sisters. Their grave is marked by a single headstone which bears their names.

founding community was risky, her brief years in the Bathurst diocese were fruitful and happy. Teresa, upon whom Aloysius had a childlike dependence, brought out the best in the young woman. Placed in charge of the first boarders to arrive at the convent, she came into her own as she cared for the children, one as young as two and a half years.[7] At times she helped in the school and often accompanied a Sister who was visiting the people in and around the village. But as Teresa's health gradually failed, Aloysius' mental state deteriorated. The uncertainty of the future and the death of her 'darling Sister Teresa' were too much for her to endure. She never recovered. One wonders what her life may have been and what further contribution she may have made to the Josephite presence in the diocese, if circumstances had been different.

During the last months of Teresa's illness, the leadership of the Sisters in the diocese increasingly rested upon Sister Joseph Dwyer. For months she faced the daily challenge of seeing the suffering of her dear friend, of trying to afford her some relief and of holding together the Sisters who felt increasingly insecure. An intelligent and astute woman, her letters to Mary MacKillop and Calasanctius Howley testify that she was well aware of what was going on around her. During the weeks before and subsequent to Teresa's death, she knew that Quinn planned to take over the Institute in the diocese and that McAuliffe had deceived the bishop regarding Mary's August visitation of the Sisters.[8] She could see Hyacinth's vacillation. She was aware that some Sisters had put about a rumour that she had treated them harshly and was unsuitable as a superior. Amid the stress of trying to steer a peaceful course through the complexity of people and circumstances, her one aim and desire was that the

---

7. Perthville Diary, 20.1.1875; 27.1.1875; Braham to MacKillop, 15.2.1875.

8. Father McAuliffe was a staunch friend to the Sisters who held him in high regard. It was he who invited Mary to hold visitation at The Vale in August 1875 and who closed the schools so that the country Sisters could attend the retreat given by Mary at the conclusion of which they renewed their vows according to the Constitutions. He also read over the formula of religious profession on the eve of the ceremony, but was not present when the Sisters renewed their vows the following morning. Later, when McAuliffe realised the anger of the bishop regarding the renewal of vows, he allowed Quinn to think that he had no knowledge of or part in Mary's visit or the Sisters' renewal of vows. He even sent a message to Mary upon her arrival in Bathurst in January 1876, requesting that she not implicate him in any way 'as to do so would cause him great trouble.' The consequence of this deception was that Quinn upbraided Mary for visiting the diocese without permission. MacKillop to Quinn, 3.2.1876.

Sisters would be loyal to Mary MacKillop and to the Constitutions. Though respectful and courteous at all times, she was not afraid of speaking the truth even to Bishop Quinn whom she set straight regarding McAuliffe's responsibility for Mary's August visit to the diocese.[9] At the same time, she was shrewd enough to know when compromise was the wisest course. Thus when directed to appoint the novices to the country convents, she did so, and when ordered away from the dying Teresa without having the comfort of a final farewell, she followed that instruction. She was indeed a capable and steadfast woman who, at the age of 25 and after just eight years in the Institute, never surrendered her responsibility for the Sisters, her adherence to truth, her self-composure or her abiding faithfulness to Mary MacKillop.[10] The following words written by one of the Sisters stationed at Borenore speak for themselves:

> We would have died in this lonely place but for the kindness of Sister M Joseph. During all her troubles she never forgot to write to us, sometimes twice a week. What she has ever been we find her still—kindness and charity to all who need her aid.[11]

It was Joseph, with Sister Francis Goodyer, who remained in the diocese to organise the other Sisters' departure, close the Wattle Flat convent and to have a final meeting with Bishop Quinn. She then returned to Adelaide. In 1884 she was appointed to Temuka in the south island of New Zealand. However, her work in New South Wales was not finished. From 1900 to 1905 she served as Provincial in Sydney. When the Sisters of St Joseph in the diocese of Wilcannia sought amalgamation with the Josephites centralised under Mary MacKillop, Joseph Dwyer was appointed by the Superior General to visit each community and arrange for the amalgamation which took place in 1902. Later, on behalf of Mary MacKillop, she also visited the new Josephite foundation in the Rockhampton diocese. She died in Sydney in 1937.

To describe Teresa's life as one signposted by a series of journeys is to encapsulate its entire breadth—both in a physical and spiritual sense.

---

9. Dwyer to MacKillop, 24.1.1876.
10. This was Joseph's age during the most difficult time at The Vale: January 1876.
11. Sister Vincent (later de Chantal) Murphy to MacKillop, 20.1.1876.

Her first journey as a small child was made from the Lowlands of Scotland to the east coast of her native land. At the age of 14 she boarded the *Sabrina* for the voyage of a lifetime—from the port of Liverpool, England to the Colony of Western Australia. There she saw the hardship of the convicts and learned that the poverty of her homeland was not overcome by the adventures of the New World. Then there was the life-determining journey to Adelaide where she met and joined the Sisters of St Joseph. After short trips within the Colony of South Australia she took the steamer to Sydney, the long train journey across the Great Divide to Bathurst and the coach trip to The Vale. From there Teresa visited Adelaide and upon her return to The Vale continued to visit the Josephite foundations made within the diocese. Though gravely ill she then made what would be her final journeys—to Trunkey Creek and back to The Vale. The stages of her life were indeed marked by the journeys of her life—from the heaving *Sabrina* atop the crest of the waves, to the dust and jostling of the coach as the horses jarred their way along the dirt track from Trunkey Creek to The Vale.

While these physical journeys set the pattern of Teresa's life, they also form the backdrop against which her inner life, her personhood, grew and matured.

When Teresa arrived in Adelaide as a young woman, she had seen a great deal of life. Caring for her little brothers and sisters, helping her mother in the running of the house, stretching the little money they had and hoping that her father would hold down his employment were experiences of the nitty-gritty of life. So were her meetings with the convicts at Guildford. So too was the frightening sea passage from Perth to Adelaide. Her ten years in Adelaide took her into colonial life and her meeting with Ellen McMullen led her to the Sisters of St Joseph. When she joined the Sisters, almost on the eve of her 29th birthday, Teresa had seen and lived life. Yet, for those who wish to know her as a person and who seek to depth her personality during those years, she has left no clues. Those twenty-nine years are in one sense unknowable.

It is only after she is settled in her first appointment away from the Franklin Street convent that the person, Teresa McDonald, comes to light. In the words and between the lines of her letters, and those of her companions, a woman emerges.

The most striking aspect of that emergence is the gradual growth to wholeness which characterised Teresa's inner journey. In her early days at Penola, she often spoke of her nothingness and of her inability to be—as she described it—'good.' Then as Provincial in Adelaide and in a difficult set of circumstances she allowed herself to be set aside by Father Woods who ignored her authority. The common sense and courage that had been evident regarding the Sisters' fasting at Kapunda, were stymied as she struggled to cope. She blamed herself for much of the disruption which occurred at that time among the Sisters. Her realisation of the gullibility of Woods in being deceived by the visionaries, and her consequent dislike of him, again led to self-recrimination. She became almost fearful of her inability to cope. But through all those troubles, Teresa learned a great deal about herself and about people. A latent ability to grasp the accuracy of a situation and to see the truth behind others' thinking and actions came to life in her. Gradually, she came into her own. With new-found strength, confidence, wisdom and courage she was well able to face and cope with the even more demanding circumstances of Mary MacKillop's excommunication. That was the woman who arrived at The Vale in 1872. She knew who she was and where she stood. Though occasionally wisdom cautioned compromise, Teresa knew how to stand her ground.

At the same time as Teresa grew in self-awareness and confidence, she wrote less and less of her failures and of her nothingness. While her letters from The Vale speak honestly of the hardship of the foundation, they are never downcast. Nor do they contain any hint of her inadequacies as Little Sister and Provincial. The experience of South Australia stood her in good stead. On her guard with Bishop Quinn, she nonetheless treated him with the utmost respect, courtesy and gratitude. No longer dependent on Father Woods, she had the confidence to seek the advice of others whom she judged more prudent and reliable than the Father Director. Even in the last days of her life, Teresa spoke confidently of the authority she held as Provincial in the Bathurst diocese. Yet, in the final months before her death, some of her old fear returned. Apprehensive of the decisions Bishop Quinn might make, she feared his presence at The Vale—especially during the last weeks of her life. Could it have been that in her gravely ill condition she doubted that she would have the strength to withstand his power regarding the Institute in his diocese?

An examination of Teresa's extant letters reveals that she rarely spoke of her loyalty to Mary MacKillop or to the Constitutions. She knew that no one required her guarantees or promises regarding the Superior General of the Institute. The fidelity she displayed as she knelt beside Mary at the time of the excommunication was proof of her faithfulness. But other Sisters afford an insight into the strength of Teresa's loyalty.[12] Joseph Dwyer knew it well. 'Sister Provincial always told us to be faithful to you, Mother, and the Constitutions.'[13] Sister Vincent (de Chantal) Murphy remembered that 'almost the last words we heard from her lips were, 'be true to our Mother House.'' Then in a reflective moment, she added: 'She died a martyr to her Holy Rule.'[14] Mary's choice of her as The Vale Provincial spoke for itself. After Teresa's death she wrote to their mutual friend, Josephine McMullen: 'We have lost our darling Sister and I firmly believe that she gave her life for her Rule and her duty.'[15]

When Sister de Sales described Teresa in her *History of the Bathurst Foundation*, she wrote that she (Teresa) 'endeared herself to all by her gentleness and kindliness of manner.'[16] This was how the Sisters remembered her—a gentle and kindly woman who maintained a compassionate and loving approach in dealing with all with whom she came in contact. It is these qualities which emerge as the hall-marks of her spirituality—compassion and love founded in humility. And it was not only the Sisters who experienced her understanding and kindness. From Penola to The Vale she reached out to the people— especially those in need—giving practical assistance when possible. As was the case with most women of her time, Teresa seemed to be able to turn her hand to whatever situation presented itself. But it was more than that. As a Sister of St Joseph she was living out that injunction of the Rule: '. . . to never see an evil without trying how they may remedy it, and thus to take a most lively interest in every external work of charity . . .'[17] Over forty years after Teresa's appointment to The Vale, Sister Mechtilde Woods drew together the qualities of her contemporary:

---

12. Letters from the Sisters to MacKillop: Francis Goodyer, Jan. 1876; Matthew Welsh, 20.1.1876; Helena Myles, 27.1.1876; Clare Kent, 27.1.1876; Stanislaus (later Immaculata) Punyer, 31.1.1876. Some Sisters changed their names after arriving in Adelaide in 1876.
13. Dwyer to MacKillop, 24.1.1876.
14. Murphy to MacKillop, 20.1.1876.
15. MacKillop to McMullen, 15.1.1876.
16. Tobin, *History*, 2.
17. Woods, *Rules of the Institute of St Joseph*, 15.

> Sister Teresa was well fitted for her new position. She was one of those favoured souls gifted with a rare piety, great prudence, with a firmness of character and gentle disposition which endeared her to all with whom she came into contact. She finally died a martyr to her Rule.[18]

For all her desire to give her life as a Sister of St Joseph, to live and work among the people, Teresa's poor health gradually prevented that wish. Again and again the Sisters' letters tell of her recurring illness. Teresa herself wrote of the severe headaches she suffered. The pain and discomfort of the primitive treatments which she underwent during the final months of her life can hardly be imagined. Unable to write letters at that stage, Teresa left no record of her final suffering. If she complained to her Sisters, they chose not to include that in their letters. The scene of her death speaks only of resignation. Hers was a life cut short. Had good health afforded her a long life, we are left to ponder what the years may have held and what might have been her ministry within the Institute.

Teresa's three and a half years at The Vale and her final illness and death can never be separated from both Bishop Quinn's determination to govern the Institute and the Sisters' resolve to remain loyal to the Constitutions. That struggle—mostly simmering below the surface but sometimes open—was the big picture against which she lived and died in the Bathurst diocese. In the end, too ill and weak to take her rightful place as Provincial, Teresa was powerless. The struggle was over. But her death leaves questions. To what extent, if any, did that struggle contribute to her illness and/or exacerbate her death? If good health had allowed her to carry out her duties as Provincial, would she have been able to negotiate with Bishop Quinn in a way that prevented the separation of the Sisters? Would the circumstances that surrounded Sister Hyacinth's decision to remain at The Vale have been averted or never have arisen? Would the diocesan Sisters of St Joseph never have been established by Bishop Quinn? The answers remain open to speculation.

Teresa's short years in the Bathurst diocese are marked by little more than her tombstone which stands in the Perthville cemetery.[19]

---

18. Mechtilde Woods, 'History', 42.
19. There is an interesting story concerning what may have been some of Teresa's belongings. About the year 1932, Sisters Winifred Turner and Laurence Morrissey found a trunk containing disintegrating clothes and some written material in the old boxroom at Perthville. After they reported it to Mothers Benedict Hickey

No photo which could be hung to commemorate her life has ever come to light. Indeed, in the years following her death, her memory among the Sisters of the Bathurst diocese faded. Yet, as the small group of Sisters of St Joseph at The Vale grew and expanded, and as the Rule amended by Father Woods for diocesan circumstances continued to be followed, a strong diocesan Congregation developed. In turn, it gave birth to other diocesan groups.[20] Teresa had laid deep foundations at The Vale—foremost among them the spirit of Mary MacKillop and Julian Woods which she learned from these co-founders. Though her memory may have faded through the years, in a sense her journey continues in the Josephite spirit that enlivens the Sisters. That is her rich legacy. She is indeed 'a priceless treasure.'[21]

Teresa of the Incarnation

---

and Joseph Mary Bowler, they later saw the two Sisters burning the contents. It is thought that the trunk contained some personal effects and letters belonging to Teresa. Apparently the trunk was with her in Trunkey Creek, returned to Perthville and stored in the old boxroom for many years. Told to Marie Crowley by Sisters Winifred and Laurence. Also see Sister Maria Joseph Looney, *Memoirs*, 7.

20. The Sisters of St Joseph in the dioceses of Goulburn, Maitland, Tasmania and Ballarat and New Zealand were founded from Perthville. In recent years the Congregations of Bathurst, Goulburn, Tasmania and New Zealand have fused (united) with the centrally governed Sisters of St Joseph, Sydney. The Sisters of St Joseph in the Maitland diocese have remained an independent Pontifical Congregation. The Sisters of St Joseph withdrew from the Ballarat diocese in 1914.

21. MacKillop to Woods, 19.9.1872.

Memoriae Sacrum

JMJ

Beautiful memory! How great is thy power,
Thy gift is more precious than gold;
One glance at thy musing in thought's pensive hour,
Would the heart's secret throbbings unfold.

From God we received thee, to Him then is due,
The first place in that all-hallowed berth;
And Mary forbids not a share, it is true
To those loved ones we've cherished on earth.

Beautiful memory, what darkens thy rays –
What cloud shades thy sunbeam of pleasure?
Alas! It is death that has snatched from thy gaze,
A friend whose worth proved her a treasure.

Oh yes! She has gone to that mansion of rest,
Where the Sisters of St Joseph inherit –
A bright crown of glory prepared for the blest,
Whose days passed in virtue and merit.

Now sadly we miss her, and silently sigh,
O'er our loss, when in grateful reflection
We think of her kindness, the heavenly tie,
That placed us beneath her protection.

In her order she shone like a heavenly star,
Showing light to the dark and deluded,
And teaching her children to praise and love God,
With their patron Saint Joseph included.

So gentle in manner, so patient and kind,
On her brow dwelt that heavenly crest,
Of interior peace, which pourtrays a pure mind,
That has charity there as its guest.

To the poor and the needy her heart opened wide,
To the orphan a motherly care;
And all who their sorrows would in her confide,
Found their trials much lighter to bear.

No wonder Saint Joseph's did sadly bewail,
And her robe of deep mourning put on;
When she heard the bells telling the sorrowful tale
That the loved Mother Teresa was gone.

Too pure for this earth, heaven claimed her her choice,
Her work in creation was done,
And death was a signal for her to rejoice,
For the bright crown of glory she'd won.

And now that she's safe o'er life's stormy sea,
And its dangers can reach her no more,
With motherly zeal she is praying that we,
Her lone children may gain heaven's shore.

Though years may roll o'er us, and grief seem to cease,
Yet for ever in memory she'll dwell,
Till we all meet again in that kingdom of peace,
Where the heart no more sorrow can tell.

Saint Joseph's.
Vale, January 13, 1876.[22]

---

22. A copy of this poem commemorating Teresa's life was found in the Perthville archives. Printed on the sheet was the following information: 'This leaflet was pasted into a prayer book used by Gertrude Abbott: "Preces Gertrudianae" (readings and prayers of St Gertrude). St Margaret's Hospital Archives.' The printing was in the hand of Sister Margaret Press who would have come across the prayer book and the poem while she was researching the history of St Margaret's Hospital subsequently published as *Sunrise to Sunrise: The History of St Margaret's Hospital Darlinghurst 1894–1994* (Sydney: Hale and Iremonger, 1994). Gertrude Abbott (the former 'visionary' Sister Ignatius O Brien) and Teresa McDonald were well known to each other from their days together in Adelaide. Given Father Woods' devotion to St Gertrude, the Latin name of the prayer book and the fact that he spent the last years of his life in the care of Gertrude Abbott and her community, it seems highly likely that the prayer book belonged to him. Gertrude would have treasured it as a keepsake of the much loved Father Director. Though the writer of the poem in honour of Teresa is unnamed, its style and wording strongly suggest that Father Woods wrote the verses in memory of her. The fact that it was found in a prayer book almost certainly belonging to him supports this supposition. The spelling 'pourtrays' in the seventh verse is the original spelling.

Bibliography

Archival Material

Archives of the Sisters of St Joseph, Adelaide.
Archives of the Archdiocese of Perth.
Archives of the Sisters of St Joseph, Perthville.
Archives of Propaganda Fide, Rome.
Catholic Parish of St John's, Portobello, Scotland.
Archives of the Sisters of St Joseph of the Sacred Heart, Sydney.

Unpublished Manuscript Sources

Book of Burials in Kulpara Cemetery, Adelaide City Council.
Certificate of Title, Register Book, vol. xvii. Adelaide City Council.
City of Adelaide Rate Assessment Book 1847–1870. Adelaide City Council.
Diary of the Sisters of St Joseph, Kapunda.
Diary of the Sisters of St Joseph, Penola.
Diary of the Sisters of St Joseph, Perthville.
Looney, Maria Joseph, *Memoirs*.
Player, Anne, *Julian Tenison Woods 1832–1889: The Interaction of Science and Religion*. Thesis submitted for the degree of Master of Arts. Australian National University. 1990.
Tenison Woods, Julian E. *Rules of The Institute of St Joseph, For The Catholic Education of Poor Children*, 1868.
---- *Explanation of the Rule and Constitution of the Sisters of St Joseph*.
Tobin, de Sales, 'History of the Bathurst Foundation', unpublished Ms.ca. 1883.

Woods, Mechtilde, 'History of the Sisters of St Joseph', unpublished Ms. ca.1918.

Newspapers

Border Watch
Freeman's Journal
Melbourne Advocate
South Australian Weekly Chronicle

Other Works

A Sister of St Joseph, *Life of Mother Mary MacKillop Foundress of the Sisterhood of St Joseph of the Sacred Heart*. Westmead, Sydney: Sisters of St Joseph, 1916.

Barker, David, (compiler) *Warders and Gaolers: A Dictionary of Western Australian Prison Officers 1829–1879* Perth: Western Australian Genealogical Society, 2000.

Byrne, Frederick, *History Of The Catholic Church in South Australia*. Adelaide: JP Hansen, 1914.

Crowley, Marie, *Women of The Vale: Perthville Josephites 1872–1972*. Richmond, Vic: Spectrum Publications, 2002.

Devine, Thomas, *The Scottish Nation 1700–2007*. London: Penguin, 2006.

Dickson, Rod. *Ships Registered in Western Australia from 1856 to 1969, Their Owners and Their Fate*. Privately published, 1956.

Foale, Marie T, *The Josephite Story: The Sisters of St Joseph: their foundation and early history 1866–1893*. Sydney: St Joseph's Generalate, 1989.

Groome, Francis, *Ordinance Gazetteer of Scotland 1882 – 1884*.

McCreanor, Sheila, (editor) *Mary MacKillop and her Early Companions: A collection of letters from 1866–1870*. North Sydney: Sisters of St Joseph of the Sacred Heart, 2013.

---- *Mary MacKillop and A Nest Of Crosses: Correspondence with Fr Julian Tenison Woods 1869–1872*. North Sydney: Sisters of St Joseph of the Sacred Heart, 2011.

McKenna, Margaret, *With Joyful Hearts! Mary MacKillop and the Sisters of St Joseph in Queensland 1870-1970*, North Sydney: Sisters of St Joseph of the Sacred Heart, 2009.

Mother Mary of the Cross MacKillop, *Julian Tenison Woods: A Life*. Canonisation edition introduced and annotated by Margaret Press rsj. Strathfield, NSW: St Pauls, 2010.

Mother Mary's Circulars to the Sisters. Sydney: Sisters of St Joseph, 1976.

Oliver, Neil, *A History of Scotland*. London: Phoenix, 2009.

O'Neil, George, *Life of the Reverend Julian Edmund Tenison Woods 1832-1889*. Sydney: Pellegrini & Co, 1929.

Press, Margaret, *From our Broken Toil: South Australian Catholics 1836-1906*. Adelaide: Catholic Archdiocese of Adelaide, 1986.

---- *Julian Tenison Woods: Father Founder*. (second edition) North Blackburn Vic: Collins Dove, 1994.

The Bicentennial Dictionary of Western Australians 1828-1888. Perth: University of Western Australia Press, 1988.

Thorpe, Osmund CP, *Mary MacKillop*, (third edition) Sydney: Sisters of St Joseph of the Sacred Heart, 1994.

Index

A

Adelaide, 1, 3, 4, 15, 16, 17, 18, 19, 20, 22, 23, 25, 26, 29, 31, 32, 36, 40, 41, 42, 43, 45, 46, 47, 50, 52, 58, 61, 63, 65, 66, 68, 69, 71, 72, 73, 74, 75, 77, 79, 81, 87, 90, 93, 98, 101, 102, 103, 106, 111, 113, 114, 116, 119, 122, 124, 126, 130, 132, 134, 135, 136, 137, 142.
Ardnamurchan, 8.

B

Borenore, 113, 114, 135.
Bowden School, 26, 32.
Braham, Ada (Sr Aloysius), 2, 78, 81.

C

Carroll, Catherine (Sr Angela), 40, 42, 44, 57, 60.
Commission of Inquiry, 77, 79, 87, 90, 93, 105, 106.
Constitutions, 111, 112, 116, 119, 120, 121, 122, 123, 124, 126, 127, 131, 132, 134, 135, 137, 138, 139.
Cunningham, Rose (Sr Rose), 25, 26, 31, 50, 58, 60, 66.

K

Kapunda, 26, 27, 29, 31, 32, 36, 37, 39, 40, 52, 54, 69, 79, 137, 143.
Kilmaurs, 10.

M

MacKillop Mary (Sr Mary), *passim.*
Markinch, 10.
McAuliffe, Rev John, 82, 83.
McDonald, Janet, 8, 9, 11, 12, 14, 15, 18.
McDonald, Margaret (Sr Teresa), *passim.*
McDonald, Martin, 8, 9, 10, 11, 12, 13, 14, 15, 17, 18, 20,
McMullen Ellen (Sr Josephine), 1, 20, 21, 23, 25, 32, 35, 50, 51, 57, 59, 62,
Mitcham Convent, 58, 62, 63, 66.
Mitcham Refuge,29, 57, 58, 59, 66.
Murphy, Bishop Daniel, 73, 74, 109.
Murphy, de Chantal (Sr Vincent), 135, 138.
Murphy, Rev Timothy, 68, 69.

N

New Perseverance, 16, 17.

O

O'Brien, Mary Jane (Sr Ignatius), 36, 42, 49,

P

Penola, 18, 19, 32, 33, 34, 35, 36, 37, 38, 39, 40, 42, 50, 51, 52, 78, 79, 137, 138, 143.
Phillips, Anna (Sr Monica), 26, 66, 68, 71, 72, 109, 112, 117.
Portobello Catholic Church, 11, 143.

CPSIA information can be obtained
at www.ICGtesting.com
Printed in the USA
FFOW04n1704030117
30973FF